HONORÉE CORDER
B.HALE

Publish
LIKE A
BOSS

FROM MIND
TO MARKET

PUBLISH
LIKE
A BOSS

FROM A WHISPER
TO A ROAR!

Paperback ISBN: 978-0-9994780-2-8

Digital ISBN: 978-0-9994780-3-5

Interior Design: Christina Gorchos, 3CsBooks.com

Honorée Corder
Ben Hale

GRATITUDE

===

From Honorée ...

Without the undying support of my husband, I wouldn't
be a writer today. Thank you for speaking words of
possibility into me every day!

Ben, what a true blessing you are! I cherish our friendship,
and our work together is so darn fun it can hardly be
called work! Thank you for inspiring me to up my writing
game and to write like a boss every day!

To my team: Christina, Dino, and Kevin—ya'll make
me look so good! Thank you for your quick and amazing
work, I'm blessed to work beside you.

From Ben ...

The list of those who have helped me is as long as my arm,
but there are certainly those who've made an enormous
difference in my career.

To Honorée, a flawless example of true friendship.

To Kathryn, my editor and ally.

And to my wife, who is perfect.

TABLE OF CONTENTS

SPECIAL INVITATION

M any like-minded individuals have gathered in an online community to share ideas, render support, and promote accountability. When I first wrote *Prosperity for Writers*, I envisioned helping numerous writers shatter the belief that they must starve to survive. I had no idea what was in store, and the result is an amazing community of 1300+ writers, authors, editors, and more!

I'd like to personally invite you to join the The Prosperous Writer Mastermind at HonoreeCorder.com/Writers and Facebook.com/groups/ProsperityforWriters where you will find motivation, daily support, and help with any writing or self-publishing questions.

You can connect with me personally on Twitter @Honoree, or on Facebook.com/Honoree. Thank you so much for your most precious resource, your time. I look forward to connecting and hearing about your book soon!

A NOTE FROM BEN

When I started writing, I knew nothing of the publishing world except that authors had agents and together they published a book, all leading to that glorious moment when a writer saw their book on the shelf of a bookstore. I had three books written when I tried to publish the first, and I sent more than a hundred query letters to agents. I thought I had written a great book and believed it deserved a chance, so I set out to get it published. How naïve I was!

After getting rejected by hundreds of agents, I began to realize it might never happen. Around this time I heard about e-publishing, the ability to publish directly to Amazon and other retailers. At first, this prospect seemed ridiculous, as if I'd be giving up. E-publishing looked like the avenue of choice for authors that couldn't publish for "real." Then I saw e-publishing for what it was: a new industry.

I devoured everything I could find on e-publishing, what many referred to as indie publishing. The ability to control my rights was appealing, and so I prepared my first book for publication, investing nearly $5,000 into editing and cover design. Five years later I've sold just shy of 200,000 copies and published seventeen books to date. But I'll leave you with a question. What would have happened if I'd held onto my previous assumptions?

A NOTE FROM HONORÉE

L ike Ben, when I first started writing I also knew nothing of the publishing world. Because I didn't have an English degree, had never taken a writing class or gained any professional credentials, it never even occurred to me to find an agent or try traditional publishing.

I had met Mark Victor Hansen, co-creator of *The Chicken Soup for the Soul* book series, at a conference I was attending. He said, "You must write a book," and I took his advice. I wrote and published my first book, *Tall Order!* (with no editing, a horrible cover, and under a different title) within a few months. It wasn't until I met the bestselling author and speaker Jeffrey Gitomer (*The Sales Bible*, among many) that I got a glimpse of what was necessary to publish a book *well*. He took one look at my freshman effort and said, "Your writing is great. This book is {bleep}!" He then introduced me to his book cover and interior designer. I took my first book and completely redid it—new cover, size, editor, and title, and then went on to sell 11,000 copies during the first three weeks.

It took many more books to find my groove and determine whom I needed on my team to turn out professionally-published books that rival the best of traditional publishers.

Although we are in the dawn of indie publishing, it is rapidly becoming a respected option for everyone. The thought that people from all walks of life and on every step of the professional ladder can write their own books and succeed thrills me to pieces. The goal Ben and I have for this book, and all three in the series, is to provide you with a reference guide that takes the guesswork out of the publishing process, leaving you with only the question, *What am I going to write?*

INTRODUCTION

Ben here! Welcome to *Publish Like a Boss*, the second in our series! This book will arm writers, aspiring authors, and published authors with the knowledge they need to publish their book professionally. Just as we did in *Write Like a Boss*, our goal is to take your book game up several notches, answer questions you didn't even know you had (and many you did but weren't sure who to ask or trust), and eliminate your blind spots.

Throughout this book, we talk about the wondrous world of publishing. It has changed a lot in recent years and is bound to change a lot more. That said, there are a lot of constants that existed before the rise of e-publishing and aren't going away anytime soon. The ability to publish directly to retailers is a tool, one that has opened new possibilities. This modern world carries a steep learning curve. The good news is you can conquer the publishing world, and if you want, you can reach the coveted yet elusive mark of full-time writer.

This book is intended as a launching point, the foundation for your career as a writer. Already know some things? Great. This book will help fill in the gaps—and trust me when I say there are thousands of pieces of information essential to building a solid career. Each can influence your success, so you may want to read even those sections you think you already understand. There's a ton of misinformation out there, and we want you to have accurate information.

One thing I'd like to stress is that this book is intended to help you master the publishing world. If you've already published several books, you might find some of the material in this book reasonably basic. Our goal here is to provide a launching point to new authors and fill in the gaps for experienced authors.

As you study the insights provided in this book, keep in mind that Honorée and I are both experienced authors with a great deal of combined knowledge. We aren't just sharing what we think works. We're sharing what we know works because we've overcome the very challenges you face.

THE C'S AND Q'S OF PUBLISHING

The new information in this book might feel overwhelming, but understanding the world of publishing is easier when you categorize the knowledge you gain. As you embark on your writing journey, you may want to classify what you learn into four distinct parts, which I call the C's and Q's of publishing.

- **Consistency.** We touched on consistent writing in *Write Like a Boss*, and here the concept continues. Consistency sets your readers' expectations and plays a hand in your publication schedule, writing style, and the types of books you publish.

- **Company.** Yes, as a writer you own your own company, hereafter referred to as your book business. Your books are products, and you are a product developer. You employ subcontractors, launch marketing campaigns, and communicate with customers, all to increase your market share and establish your brand.

- **Quality.** Writing quality content is essential to a career, and we talked a lot about this in *Write Like a Boss*. Keep in mind that quality writing will draw readers back, not bring in new ones. They haven't read it yet!

- **Quantity.** Writing a lot is crucial to building a writing career. One book is unlikely to set you for life, nor are two or three. If your goal is to write full-time, then quantity is going to help you get there.

As you read this book, consider what you learn in the context of these four elements. Ask yourself, *Does this apply to my company? Or to increasing my quantity?* Whether you are traditional or indie publishing, you may wear multiple hats: the writer, the publisher, the marketer, and the business expert. All these roles require knowledge and discipline. The C's and Q's of writing will help you target the areas that need your focus.

Publishing like a boss is about mastering all aspects of publishing and positioning yourself and your books where you and they can succeed. Let's use an analogy to illustrate this.

I grew up in a family of boys, three to be exact. Despite this, my brothers and my dad didn't like to play or watch sports, meaning that we watched a lot of *Star Trek*. (Not that *Star Trek* is bad!) I loved sports but had a hard time learning to play because of the lack of experience.

I would frequently play with a few friends at our church, but because I didn't know what to do, I would often spend an entire game without touching the ball. Looking back, I was seriously terrible, so I shouldn't have been surprised that my friends were reluctant to give me the ball. Still, I was discouraged by this lack of playing time and complained once to a friend. His response proved to be more profound than I think he ever imagined.

"Get open, and the ball will come to you."

I was surprised by his answer, but even more surprised that it worked. When I was blatantly open, my friends would occasionally pass me the ball, and I began to improve. My desire to play increased, and I practiced at home, excited to get even better. Even without help from my family, I became a decent basketball player.

Becoming a full-time, publishing-like-a-boss, six-figure-earning writer is about *mastery*. Your odds of success are slim when you are stationary because success won't just come to you. You have to move, learn, and work as you invite success to come to you.

The fact that you are reading this book demonstrates your desire to learn and grow, or in other words: "get open." Every piece you master helps you get past barriers and prevents future mistakes, pushing you toward your dreams. We can't force your success (as much as we'd like to!), but we can help you make it happen for yourself.

We've been where you are, and we know the challenges and doubts you must overcome. As you dive into this book, we hope you will see the steps that will bring you to what you desire most. Get open, and success will come to you.

Defining *Like a Boss*

Honorée here: There are several schools of thought about how authors should publish, and I'm not one to argue when someone's mind is made up. I sometimes see sketchy, frightening, and not-so-good practices I know will create problems in the future. Publishing like a boss means having the mentality of a business owner. It means treating each book as a product and producing it with quality and forethought. It also means your product looks the part—in the case of publishing, it means you professionally publish your books.

I *must* open this section by saying your book has to come as close to looking like it was produced by a traditional publishing house as possible. Prepare to invest both time *and money* in your book business. Every successful business employs a team to help it flourish. Traditional businesses need support staff and management, with each person focusing their expertise to help the business grow. There is often a social media or marketing expert, someone in finance or accounting, and a legal department.

Your book business, if not now then eventually, will need its own cast of characters: the writer (that's you!), an editor, a proofreader, a cover designer, a copywriter, and an interior designer (formatting)—and, please note, *these people are not you!* Unless, before right now, you have training in these areas or are a self-taught professional (i.e., your tax return says "graphic designer" or "editor"), you must plan to pay and pay well for these services.

Ben here: I'd like to jump in here if I may. I agree with Honorée about identifying the group of individuals you need to publish your book. However, the list can be highly specific based on your project. One might need an illustrator, editor, and cover designer, while another might need an editor, cover designer, book coach, copywriter, and interior designer. What's important is that you identify the elements you need to make your book great. That said, nearly everyone needs an editor, copywriter, and cover designer. Your high school English teacher may be an excellent person, but may not be the best individual to help you produce a book that looks flawless.

Honorée here: Don't worry; we'll help you learn how to identify these key players.

Let me come at this another way: I see five significant mistakes when it comes to publishing books. Each one of these mistakes can be avoided! I'm not calling anyone out in these pages, nor do I sit on a throne of judgment. I believe Oprah said it best, "When we know better, we do better." I want you to know how to do each aspect of your business well so you can be successful and *Publish Like a Boss*. In other words, this is the fastest path to becoming a full-time, successful writer.

I've made these mistakes (in spades) and many more. And I didn't start making real, consistent money until I began to treat my book business the way I operated my network marketing business, my coaching business, and my speaking business: like it was a *business*.

Mistake #1: Being cheap.

I'm a little on my soapbox for this first point because I see far too many people trying to get their books produced on the cheap—covers through Fiverr or from sub-par designers. Using their street team (also known as their *advanced reader team*) as their editors. Throwing up any old blurb and back cover copy. Just so they can avoid spending money.

This, my friends, is a huge symptom of a poverty consciousness. If your first consideration is money and how much you are spending, kindly take a step back and decide if being an author is going to be a hobby or business. A business requires an investment, a capital investment. You will need to invest money into your book business if you expect to see a high ROI (return on investment). Very rarely does a poorly edited book with a crappy cover become a runaway hit or an international bestseller (I can't name even one, can you?).

It may seem as though I'm taking a hard line here, and I am. I took shortcuts and tried to get away with not paying a fair wage for a great job. And my books suffered, and therefore, *my sales suffered.* I want you to set the expectation that you're going to pay for quality editing and proofreading (*not* by the same person), hire a talented designer to do your covers, engage the services of a bona fide copywriter for your book description, and get your book formatted by a professional. All so your book, one of zillions of books, will *stand a chance.* So it could become a runaway hit or an international bestseller, impacting the lives of thousands, hundreds of thousands, or, God willing, millions of people.

Trust me: okay is not good enough! You put enough time, energy, sweat, and tears into your books that they deserve to have the polish of an experienced editor, a proofreader with a keen eye, and a professionally-designed cover.

You may have to wait so you can save up to pay for these services. You *might* be able to find talented individuals who don't charge a lot for great work. And I'm all for a bargain. Just today my daughter and I went back-to-school shopping and we were *giddy* to find the cutest jumpsuit (ever!) for only $12.99 (80% off)! But quality folks charge quality prices for quality work. That's just the way it goes.

Mistake #2: Rushing.

The sister mistake of being cheap is rushing to publish. Quality books that sell require time. I understand all too well that writing and finishing the last ten percent of the book feels like the last fifty percent. You cannot wait to press the publish button, hold your book in your hot little hands, and refresh your sales data all day long the first week after launch.

Trust me when I say there is plenty to do even as your book is in the editing, proofreading, and formatting stages (such as setting up your social media platforms, building your email list, scheduling podcast interviews, possibly starting your own podcast, and networking and building relationships with other authors). You need to build time into your production schedule to read and re-read your manuscript to ensure it does what you want it to do (I'll talk more about what goes into your book, and what doesn't, shortly).

We talked about the draft process in *Write Like a Boss*. When your book is with your editor, beta readers, or ART, that isn't time off from your business! It's time to do other types of work that are just as essential to building your brand. Publishing like a boss is understanding that product development is much more than just the product.

Just as you must understand there's a substantial financial investment you'll need to make in each book in your book business, you'll also need to pump the brakes and give each step in the process the amount of time it needs.

Mistake #3: Having no long-term vision.

I'm often asked, "How does someone become an Amazon bestseller?"

Answer: it isn't hard at all.

With less than a dozen book sales in the same hour, you can crush it and become #1 in your (most likely) obscure category on Amazon. Price your book at a reasonable $6.99, and you've made less than $50 for all your time, effort, and investment.

Not what you had in mind, I'm sure. Not what I have in mind, without question!

Better question: "How does someone write a best-*earning* book?"

I'm so glad you made this distinction. Many early authors I meet are focused on sales and promotion. Although these are important aspects, they are only part of a longer-term perspective. Is your goal to sell books? Or make a living? Make sure your short-term choices align with your long-term goals.

Each of my books has one purpose and three interconnected goals: to reach as many readers as possible, help as many people as possible, and earn as much as possible.

With that in mind, I strategically design, write, edit, and publish each book with the help of a highly-skilled team, all while keeping an eye on the time, money, energy, and effort I put into it. If you want a book that boosts your brand, increases your business, and helps you become the go-to expert (as well as a book that makes money from now until long after you've left this planet), you need to observe the same publishing principals.

Decide before you begin writing what your desired outcome is for the book (and for each one you write). Will it help you boost your brand? Do you want your book to replace your business card and help you attract more clients? Do you want to create an income stream from your books? All of the above? None of the above?

A long-term vision for your book business is the key to your long-term success. Defining your vision *now* will help you to stay focused when those around you are getting distracted by what's hot in the moment. I'm clear about what I want from my book business this year, next year, and five years from now—and as a result, every step I take brings me closer to my desired outcome. I stay focused, productive, and positive and I don't (under any circumstances) take a wild left turn because the herd does. Neither should you.

Mistake #4: Failing to establish a brand.

Before you even write the first word of your outline, write down a clear description of your current business brand. What exactly do you offer, and to whom? What are the standards for your brand? What are you passionate about? How you see yourself is not always how others see you (especially if you make mistakes #1, #2, and #3). We dive into branding in the next book in this series, *Market Like a Boss*.

I offer quality, no-nonsense advice and coaching to select individuals who want to write, publish, and launch a best-selling *and* best-earning book. That's my brand. To that end, I also write books that offer quality, no-nonsense advice to individuals who want to write, publish, and launch best-selling *and* best-earning books.

I don't compete with those who *say* they are experts. I just continue to produce great-quality books, build my brand, and raise my profile. When you're the best, you stand out. Aren't *you* the best? Isn't that why you want to publish a book that showcases your knowledge and expertise and helps you to attract more clients and customers who want exactly what you're selling? I would imagine so.

Mistake #5: Not creating a long-term business plan.

This mistake is part of a necessary and more significant discussion, which is included in *Market Like a Boss*.

However, here's what will fit in perfectly here: taking a step back to figure out (a) your longer-term business plan and (b) how a book (or more than one book) fits into that plan is critical to your overall and long-term success.

I see far too many people write and publish books without thinking through how the book fits into their business or even how to design the contents of the book for maximum benefit. Just having a book is not enough if it doesn't work hard on your behalf. You want a book to help people solve their problem and prove your expertise.

Before you write the first words of your book, be sure to answer the question: *What do I want my reader to do, not do, or both as a result of reading my book?* For this book, we want readers to publish their books and know how to do it professionally. We don't want readers to make the same mistakes we've made or that we've seen others make.

Now that you know the five mistakes, you're going to be sure to avoid them. Now that we've trudged through the mud a little, I want to focus on the good stuff, the fun stuff. Let's do that, shall we?

THE BASICS OF PUBLISHING

Ben here: Publishing has radically changed in the last decade. The advent of e-publishing has permanently altered the industry and will continue to have a lasting impact. Regardless of your individual opinions about publishing, it's vital we start with the basics. You can't "publish like a boss" unless you understand the publishing market.

There are five main ways you can publish a book, each with advantages and disadvantages. Before you ask, one is not better than another. What matters is that you pick the route that's right for you—and you can't know that unless you understand them all.

TRADITIONAL PUBLISHING

Today's traditional publishing market is a vast network of companies, imprints, and smaller presses. The five largest publishing houses are called the Big Five, and they control many smaller entities as well as much of the market. All have different submission requirements, but most do not allow authors to query them directly.

Authors seeking publication typically pursue literary agents using the all-important query letter. Although each agent and agency has different submission requirements, nearly all require a one-page letter detailing the premise of the book and the author's writing history. The query letter is more art than science, and we could write an entire book on how to query an agent. Unfortunately, the process is so unique and changes so often that such a book would be obsolete in a year. You can find all the information you need on this topic with a simple internet search.

Many agents receive hundreds of query letters per day, and this stack of submissions is referred to as the "slush pile." Because so many queries are received, agents use every excuse to discard them. Of the few that stand out, one or two may be accepted for representation. And this is just the first hurdle for aspiring authors.

Armed with an agent, authors begin submitting their work to publishers, who have their own slush piles. An editor selects a few works among many.

Books selected for publication typically go through a two-year process of preparation and editing (even your previously-edited book) before the book is published. Statistically, new authors don't sell well, and the ones that don't are dropped by the publisher, and possibly the agent. Some become "mid-listed," meaning they sell enough to keep around, but not enough for the publishers to put much money into marketing. An exceptional few sell enough to make publishing a full-time occupation.

Author's initial investment: almost zero. Agents only take a percentage of what a writer receives. The same applies to publishers. The advance for new authors is about $5,000 on average. Beyond that, royalties (greatly simplified) are about 10% of retail price. To earn a living, an author would need to sell more than 200,000 books per year to earn approximately $60,000 (US). Not a bad income, without question, but selling that many books is rare for most authors.

The work required by the author is more than many realize. In the current market, authors are required to blog, hang out on Facebook, pay for their advertising, and do multiple other activities and events to promote their work. Only the highest-selling authors get extensive marketing aid. Many traditionally-published authors must also write two to three books a year to make a living.

The time required to publish is typically two years (this is fast-tracked if you can believe it) to as many as two decades. Yes, it can take a long time to gain an agent, and then more time to get accepted by a publisher. Once a publisher accepts you, it typically takes another two years before the book is released. Some authors get signed to an agent but ultimately get dropped because the agent can't get a publisher to bite, hence the possibility of decades.

Honorée here: One of my book coaching clients spent six months working with an agent, with no book deal in sight *even though* said agent was excited about her book! The cost of this delay: tens of thousands of dollars in book sales income as well as other lost revenue due to her lack of a book. The ultimate price paid: incalculable.

You can tell I have always been and remain a fan of indie publishing, and you'll be happy to know a lot is coming up on that subject.

Ben again: Traditional publishing may seem daunting, but the potential rewards can be significant. There are still many awards available only to traditional authors, and some of the major bestseller lists heavily favor traditionally-published authors.

I've met authors that are traditionalists to the core and believe it to be the only route to publication. If you are one of these, try to keep an open mind in the next few sections. You may be surprised.

INDEPENDENT PUBLISHING

Independent publishing is still traditional in most respects, but it has enough distinctions that it merits its own category. An independent publisher operates much like a traditional publisher but seeks queries directly from authors. These smaller presses have looser guidelines that make it easier to publish, but with the caveat that they lack the reach or experience of a larger imprint.

Many independent presses don't require an agent, and their terms are frequently more favorable than one of the big New York presses. They are smaller, sometimes with a fraction of the staff to work on an author's project. Others are nearly as large as Penguin and Random House but still focus on a smaller market. The variety of independent publishing houses permits a variety of authors to publish, and there is always a press that works in a particular genre.

The disadvantage of independent presses is their reach. They lack the resources of larger imprints, so they may not offer foreign translations, audiobooks, or editorial work. Their marketing team may lack experience, and their advances are typically much smaller. Note that not all independent publishing firms place books into bookstores, potentially removing one of the primary motivators for an author to choose this avenue. The time from contract to publication is usually shorter, but the author will still shoulder the brunt of the marketing efforts.

One type of independent publishing is through Amazon, which now has its own imprints. These invite-only presses offer greater marketing potential to authors. Amazon's imprints are a prime example of this publishing route. They have a specific reach and unique parameters and are not as large as the traditional publishing houses.

They also seem to be a rapidly-rising niche compared to other publishing types.

Independent houses have a great deal of potential and may fit your situation and what you hope for your writing. They tend to adapt more quickly than the larger houses, and many imprints are capitalizing on the exact tools useful to indie authors. The sheer number of independent presses, however, makes a comprehensive conversation difficult.

Independent publishing is where many authors get their start. Armed with publications from a smaller press, an author may appear more appealing to a larger house. However, proceed with caution when approaching smaller presses. Not all have quality business practices, so don't jump at the first sign of interest from an imprint.

If you think an imprint, or any company, might be a good fit, take some time and do due diligence. Ask for references, talk to other authors who have used their services. Make sure they've been in business for a while (more than five years is ideal), have a substantial and current web presence, etcetera.

SELF-PUBLISHING

Many call self-publishing "vanity publishing." The self-publishing process is perceived as negative for many publishers, writers, and readers. Whereas traditional publishing has several barriers to prevent poor quality work from being released, self-publishing has none. When it comes right down to it, a self-publishing company charges authors to print their books. Nearly all sell services such as editing, cover design, and marketing wrapped into packages that cost between $500 to $10,000 (or more). These companies are essentially functioning as printers. They claim they will publish professionally and market for success, but few fulfill their promises.

It's important to note that self-publishing houses make their money from the authors instead of the royalties. The distinction may seem small, but self-publishing houses do not care if you sell books primarily because they make their money from you. If it's not clear already, I have no love for self-publishing houses. Learn to recognize them so you can avoid them.

There's a great site called Editors and Predators that lists a few of the many self-publishing companies with questionable business practices. If you are offered a contract—especially if it stipulates that you are to pay for services—check the site for information on the company. You can avoid a great deal of heartache with just a few minutes of research.

If you receive an offer, always verify the source. Companies regularly prey on authors who don't understand the system, so don't fall for their seedy practices. Even if the publishing house isn't listed on Editors and Predators, search into their history and look up books they have published. How high are their *books* ranked on Amazon? How high are their *authors* ranked on Amazon? (Information on rankings is later in this book, as well as in *Market Like a Boss*.) Are the books selling? How many reviews do they have and how are they reviewed (lots of verified 5-star reviews or not)? Ask for the contact information of happy clients and spend the time reaching out to have a conversation or two. Ask the tough questions and make sure you've found a reputable company.

A few years ago, I met an author who had paid $10,000 to a company to publish her book. It was a children's book, so formatting mattered! Each page needed a specific layout to look right. She received forty copies of a book that was formatted incorrectly, with misplaced text, color mistakes, and poorly-constructed bindings. She rightfully complained, but the company claimed they had delivered the products as promised. Their "professional marketing services" amounted to nothing, and this author was left with forty copies of a book she couldn't sell. Unfortunately, stories like this are all too common. Honorée has one as well:

> I recently spoke to a writer's special interest group. After I had been speaking for about twenty minutes, one lovely woman broke down in tears. She produced her book, which had a typo *on the cover*. She had paid $22,000 for her book. It had a terrible cover (in addition to the egregious error), the interior formatting was horrible, and worst of all, they had shipped her books late—so she had no books at her book launch party! It cost her a few thousand dollars to get her book edited, reformatted, and a new cover designed so she could use the book for her originally-intended purposes. She's on track now, but what an expensive and stressful situation!

Ben here: If anyone in the publishing industry wants to charge you for a service, especially to publish, always verify the source. Although I cannot say with 100% certainty that all self-publishing houses are scams, I can say with certainty to keep your guard up. Be wary of those that seek to take advantage of you. Your book deserves better. You deserve better.

INDIE PUBLISHING

Indie publishing refers to authors who act as their own publishers. Some call this self-publishing, and in the strictest sense, it is. However, indie authors don't use another company to publish their books; they do every aspect of the publishing process (contracting for editing, proofreading, formatting, and cover design, as well as creating accounts on online retailers and uploading the finished product) themselves.

Digital books are usually the primary focus of indie authors and are the core of their marketing efforts. The printed books they do sell are "print on demand," meaning a single book is printed and shipped when an order is received. Indie authors do not tend to order large shipments of books and try to sell them. Instead, they do most of their work and promotion online (at home in their pajamas—or is that just Honorée?).

The downside to indie publishing is the initial cost, both in money and time. You will need an editor, a cover designer, and possibly other services such as formatting or book coaching (which Honorée beautifully provides to a small, select group of clients).

Some indie authors don't use a professional editor and upload their book to Amazon "as is." This trend has helped foster a stigma that indie books are poorly edited and written. More prepared authors invest in their books to give them the best chance at success.

The good news is that authors can expect to publish virtually for free. Publishing on Amazon, the iBookstore, Kobo, and other sites is free. And the royalties are very favorable. Authors can expect to receive upwards of 70% of their sales. A $3 book nets you about $2. A couple of dollars per sale might not seem like a lot, but those royalties quickly add up as your sales rack up!

Successful indie authors work hard to grow their business and brand. Doing so requires dedication. Some indie authors devote little time to their digital books, allowing the sales and growth to generate their own momentum. Others allocate more time to actively marketing. Either way, it is up to authors to choose how much time they want to invest.

Once finished, all the book needs are a cover and a book description. It takes less than eight hours to format a book to publish (unless you use a professional formatter—more on that later). All that is left is to upload it, which takes a few minutes of filling in the blanks. Online retailers require just a few pieces of information (author's name, book title, etc.) in addition to your finished manuscript and book cover.

We'll go into much greater detail about indie publishing in chapter 2, so for now let's move on to the final publishing avenue.

HYBRID PUBLISHING

Hybrid publishing is another sub-route that deserves its own category. Authors who publish this way *blend* two of the above mentioned options into their publication strategy. Being a hybrid author allows them to balance the benefits and drawbacks of two different publication types. For example, an author with three traditionally-published books and four that are indie published is likely to see greater overall revenue and a larger readership than authors using just one or the other.

While new writers are more likely to look at the previous four routes of publication, experienced authors are more likely to consider hybrid publishing. Because of the dual roles, a basic understanding is a prerequisite, and a steep learning curve should be expected. This route is newer than the others, but more and more authors are leaning toward a hybrid model to reach their goals.

The interesting thing about hybrid publishing is that authors from both traditional and indie are moving in the opposite direction. I've met traditionally-published authors that switched to indie for their new books. I've also met indie authors using their sales and readership to make the jump to traditional. Large houses love to see an author willing to write, learn, and publish. They will likely not be interested in your already-published content, but they will be involved in helping you make more sales. In this regard, going the indie route can be a stepping stone to traditional, if that's your goal.

About three years ago, I read a story of an author in California with six published novels. She'd used two small publishing houses which had published three each. In her own words, she was hanging on "by the skin of her teeth." Then she learned she was being dropped for lack of sales by her second publisher.

She was rightfully devastated and wondered how she could support herself financially. Then she got angry and considered indie publishing for the first time. Within a year of publishing her first indie novel, she'd earned eight figures. That's over ten million dollars!

Going back to the C's and Q's I mentioned in the introduction, she had quality, quantity, and consistency. She made a company decision that sent her earnings into the stratosphere. That's the power of hybrid publishing. Blending the benefits of two types of publishing can drastically increase your readership.

If you do go hybrid from traditional, make sure to read your contracts carefully. Many traditional houses have a clause that you cannot indie publish books from the world or series you publish with them. They might even say you cannot use the same author name, which would mean starting from scratch. If you are reading this book and have a publishing contract offer, read it carefully so you can keep your options open. Most houses offer a standard contract to start and at the author's request will remove specific clauses.

If you are going from indie to traditional, keep the same cautions in mind. The traditional publishing house may want the rights to your author name, the brand, the designs, and perhaps even your website. They may say you can't indie publish within three months of a traditional book coming out, which can severely hurt your ability to be a hybrid. This route of publishing can be tremendous, but just make sure you approach it cautiously.

But which publishing option is best for you?

Asked by every writer who is just starting out, and the only answer comes from within each writer. Every author, their work, and their life is so unique it is impossible to choose which is better than another. (Except self-publishing, which is usually bad for all!) Like all of you, I learned of traditional publishing first, and considered it the sole avenue to publication. But when I learned of indie publishing, I knew it was the best fit for me. I wanted to be in control, to manage my own content, to direct my own fate. Learn them all, and then choose which option fits you best.

I think that the question of indie versus traditional comes down to your goals. If your goal is to build a six-figure income, indie publishing is likely the stronger candidate. If you like to learn and enjoy controlling your own content, you also might lean toward indie.

On the other hand, if you don't care to learn all the ins and outs of indie publishing or are too busy to write consistently, then traditional may be the option for you. The additional time it takes for a publishing house to bring a book to market might fit perfectly into your schedule.

One caveat! Many authors think that publishing traditionally means they won't have to market their book, and all they will have to do is sit back and watch the royalties roll in. If only! In actuality, the opposite is true. Unless you are selling incredibly well, traditional houses don't set up book tours, don't do online marketing, and don't pay for marketing services. But they will deduct anything they spend off the top before you earn any money. A tiny percentage of traditionally-published authors make a living on which they can live.

Both indie and traditional publishing will require you to run your business, market your work, understand business taxes, etc. If you expect a big imprint to handle all that for you, you might never get a contract that will truly help you meet your goals.

YOU ARE THE BOSS!

Regardless of the route you ultimately choose, never forget that fact. All of the ways we've mentioned are viable when done correctly, so it only matters what you think will be the best fit with you and your book business.

Most important of all, don't let indecision keep you from acting. This book will help you prevent many common mistakes, but you cannot avoid every single one. And that's okay! I look back and cringe at the mistakes I made, and I did hundreds of hours of research. Still, those mistakes helped shape my career, teaching me what I needed to grow. Remember, publishing like a boss is a journey that starts with your first publication. Will it be perfect? Maybe, maybe not, but it's the first step towards the ideal book release. (I'm not there yet!)

Once you've made your decision, gather your courage and push forward. A career of one hundred books starts with a single book release.

Indie publishing—and especially indie publishing on Amazon—is an industry. It's still evolving. As you prepare yourself to enter the market, I highly recommend you study as much as you can on nearly every topic. Small details can make an enormous difference in your strategy and plan. Luck may play a hand in your ultimate success, but you can stack the odds in your favor.

PUBLISHING ETIQUETTE

Publishing will bring your life into the public sphere, and there are a few nuances of which you need to be aware. Here are a few things you need to know.

1. **Double-check Your Facts.** The author is always the ultimate one responsible for accuracy in their books, not the publisher. If you traditionally publish, you may get assistance, but the responsibility ultimately falls on you. If you're going to reference exact places, people, or events, do your homework. Eagle-eyed readers will call you on mistakes or post harsh reviews if you use incorrect information.

2. **Have Cultural Sensitivity.** Be mindful when referencing cultures, religions, races, countries, and politics. In nonfiction books, you have an opinion—you are the author, after all! But be aware your reader may have an entirely different

view on the subject, and you don't want to offend or hurt someone (unless you intend to be controversial). Fiction books have villains that must come from somewhere, but disparaging an entire community can come back to haunt you.

3. **You're in the Public Eye Now, Baby!** We'll explore this more in-depth later, but want to touch on it here later, but we want to touch on it here. Being a published author means you stand in the public's eye. Posting about hot-button topics like politics is fine when people have no way to reach you and no way to retaliate. But when you have published a book, people will sometimes give harsh criticism of your book. We're not saying you have to keep your opinions to yourself; we're saying be smart about what you post. Make sure you think through the possible consequences that may come with your posts and views.

Now that we've covered the basics, we're ready to dive into the meat of the issue. The next chapter goes into detail on indie publishing. There are hundreds of pieces to this exciting new world, and Honorée and I both love to talk about it, so let's get going, shall we?

2

INDIE PUBLISHING:

A Closer Look

The Indie Publishing World Today: A Snapshot

Ben here: In just a few short years, indie publishing has become a juggernaut. Hundreds of thousands of authors have used the publication tools of Amazon, Kobo, iBooks, Sony, and others. Indie writers have a presence on bestseller lists—and not just the obscure genre lists. *The New York Times, USA Today*, and the *Wall Street Journal* have all seen indie writers appear on their prestigious lists.

Once heralded as a gimmick, indie publishing has grown to rival the whole of traditional publishing. Don't believe me? Just look at a site called Author Earnings Report. They do statistical studies on sales and publishing, and their results are mind blowing. Want to know which genre makes more in sales? They have a report for that. Want to know if there's an increase in indie or traditional authors making a million dollars or more? They have a report for that.

Indie authors now have titles translated into foreign markets, placed in bookstores, and released as audio books. Indie authors like Hugh Howey were the first to shatter the ceiling, and many have followed their examples. Now indie authors are spreading into games, television, and even film.

I provide for my family of eight purely from the royalties of my books, and I'm hardly the minority. I've met hundreds of authors who write full-time, and nearly all went through the same process as I did. You want to publish like a boss and become a full-time writer? Here's your chance. The industry is ready for you.

Honorée here: I, too, am a successful indie author earning six figures from my royalties each year. While Ben and I have traversed very different routes, we have both ended up as indies and love it!

DIGITAL PUBLISHING: THE WORKS

Ben here: There are now many digital bookstores where you can buy or sell ebooks. Amazon is the largest, with the Nook program second in the United States. The iBookstore has a more global reach and, depending on the content, can be a better fit. Other retailers like Sony, Kobo, Diesel, Draft2Digital, and others have also opened their respective doors, allowing anyone to publish their content direct to market.

Amazon is the largest book retailer in the world, and their publishing platform is robust and easy to use. The site is Kindle Direct Publishing, or KDP. The dashboard showing your royalties is particularly useful. It also has several help pages and resources available to walk you through the process.

There are several things you'll need to publish on any digital retailer, and it is best to come prepared. Here's a handy list:

An Edited Manuscript.

As an indie, no one looks at your book before publication. Readers will be the first to decide if it's well written. It's easy to make the mistake of thinking your book is perfect and publishing without hiring a good editor—don't!

Honorée here: There are those who use alternate methods to eliminate mistakes from their books, in lieu of hiring an editor. I cannot stress enough how important it is to have a professional editor (their tax return says "Editor" in the profession box) do at least one round of edits of every book you intend to publish. A second look from a professional in the form of a final proofread is also a great idea.

Cover.

We highly recommend you hire an artist or graphic designer to do professional design work. With professional design, you get a better-quality cover, and you own the rights to the image. The two hallmarks of a good cover are sharp color contrast and clarity. Keep in mind that your readers will likely be viewing your book on a phone, so your cover will be the width of your finger. We'll go into more detail on covers in *Market Like a Boss.*

Your book never gets a second chance to make a first impression! A great cover creates interest and encourages potential readers to find out more. Once they take a look, you'll need an excellent book description to close the deal.

Book Description/Blurb/Sales Copy.

Ben here: Many authors abhor writing their blurb, so they don't take the necessary care to write copy that sells. This mistake can cost you a great deal in the short- and long-term. The cover causes people to look at the book. (Online, this means they will feel compelled to click on it.) But the description sells the book. I shudder when I see long book descriptions riddled with typos. I prefer to write my own, but a good copywriter can do one for you.

Consider hiring a professional copywriter to do a top-shelf book description or read Joe Sugarman's *The Adweek Copywriting Handbook* so you can master sales copy yourself.

Honorée here: Or both! As a boss, you need to have a working knowledge of all aspects of your business.

Understanding the philosophy and formula behind great copywriting can only help you refine good copy to make it great. The book description our hired copywriters craft is based on pieces of information about our books, but rarely do they read them in their entirety (in fact, I don't think that has ever happened). You want to make sure the final copy accurately reflects your book, and a keen understanding of copywriting combined with intimate knowledge of your book can amplify your description.

Title.

Ben here: "Have an incredible title" might seem obvious, but there's more to it than just picking any title for your book. Go to Amazon and search for your working title. You may find that your perfect title is the same as a book in a vastly different genre, with a vastly different audience. Books with the same title are fine unless you're writing the exact same type of book. Then you'll want to choose a different one. Check the other titles before you decide.

A fiction title can be tricky because it's likely linked to your brand. It's wise to do some research before settling on a title or book series name. If yours is nearly identical to other books, that could cause your book to underperform. If it's too confusing, it could underperform. Your title should be clear and connected to your brand.

When I was going to publish a short story prequel for my series, I wanted to title it *The Swordsman*, because the book is about an assassin with that name. But when I did research, my title was used almost exclusively in kung fu literature and movies. My book would not have fit in at all! A little more research and I titled it, *Assassin's Blade*. A quality title can play a significant part in how your book performs.

Honorée here: In nonfiction, the title is the *what*: what is the main subject of the book? The subtitle is the *promise*: what will the reader "get" (what are the benefits) in exchange for buying and reading the book. Example: *The Four-Hour Work Week: Escape the 9-5, Live Anywhere, and Join the New Rich*. There is much more about this in chapter 4: "Publish Nonfiction Like a Boss."

Price.

Pricing a book also seems straightforward, but I've met many authors who were dead set on pricing their fiction ebook at $8. Unless you have a massive, devoted following, this will kill your sales. Most indie authors agree that ebooks should be between $2.99 and $5.99, with the caveat that short fiction might be $0.99. Look for comparable books if you aren't sure.

Pricing your nonfiction book is a little bit of a different animal. Nonfiction solves a problem and provides valuable information for a fraction of what it would cost to hear it straight from the expert. Therefore, nonfiction books can be priced higher, between $6.99 and $9.99 for ebooks, and $14.99 to $19.99 for print editions.

You might notice our *Like a Boss* nonfiction books are priced lower. This is because the lower price makes sense in the market for books about writing and writers.

It is a great idea to give away a short ebook, or even price it at $0.99, to give potential readers a glimpse of the knowledge you possess. Again, I'll talk more about how to price your book in chapter 4: "Publish Nonfiction Like a Boss."

Keywords.

Keywords can be tricky, and we'll go into much more detail about them in *Market Like a Boss*. Keywords are text tags that identify your book as relevant in a search; they are phrases rather than just a single word (although they *can* be single words). You can find your own by mining the Amazon search bar, or you can use products like Kindle Spy, Kindle Samurai, or KDP Rocket. For Amazon, you'll need seven keywords, and remember one keyword equals a string of words. For example, one of my keywords is "Action and Adventure Trilogies."

Identifying the best keywords for your nonfiction book is essential, more so than you might think. When someone is searching for a book to solve a problem, they don't have any idea what is available or the best book for their situation. The right keywords can place your book at the top of the search results, causing more sales, which increases the book's (and your author) rank, which leads to more long-term sales. I share the least you need to know about keywords in chapter 4: "Publish Nonfiction Like a Boss."

PUBLISH LIKE A BOSS

Publishing Your Book: Online Retailers

Amazon may be the biggest online retailer (including for books), but there are many digital retailers to consider, and each one has their own challenges and benefits. They may have different formatting or upload requirements, and they often cater to different demographics. We could go into an exhaustive description of the specific upload procedures, but that is exactly what it would be: *exhausting*. Just be prepared for a slight learning curve with each one.

Below is a brief list of some of the larger retailers with their associative benefits and drawbacks. To fully understand them will require more research, but this will give you a starting point. To *publish like a boss*, you should know your retailers, so let's dive in:

Barnes and Noble has their own indie publishing platform, NookPress. It lacks the depth of Amazon but has useful features like the ability to make changes in the text while online. Barnes and Noble obviously has a greater connection with print books, so if you want to sell more print copies, Barnes and Noble may be a retailer you want to include in your publishing efforts. In today's market, Barnes and Noble's customers like to visit the physical bookstores while browsing the website, allowing them to purchase ebooks that catch their eye.

One caveat with NookPress is that at the time of this writing, it looks to be in the process of being eliminated. It's only existed for a few years, so this highlights the highly volatile nature of the current publishing world.

The iBookstore from Apple is indeed a global marketplace. Publishing in the iBookstore requires a Mac computer. You simply download their program to your computer, then you prepare your book for upload. Another exciting feature of the iBookstore is the ability to allow your books to be pre-ordered a full year in advance. Not that you necessarily should do it, but it's an option.

Kobo is a rising star based in Canada. Its reach may be smaller in the United States, but that doesn't mean you shouldn't include it on your list. I've met some of Kobo's executive team, and they are smart and dedicated to their authors and the author experience. Their dashboard is called Kobo Writing Life, and it is easy to use and understand. Unlike Amazon, you can publish free books. We'll go into why and when to do free books in *Market Like a Boss*.

We've touched on three of the largest retailers outside of Amazon, but there are a dozen more, each catering to smaller, niche markets. To upload a single book to all of these is a challenge, but when you have ten books it's a nightmare, especially when you use live links.

Important! Live links can be embedded into your digital book so readers can quickly and easily find your other books. This is essential and incredibly easy. But just imagine trying to keep your content up to date across all your books and all retailers. The good news is that the next three companies have a shortcut.

Smashwords, although relatively unknown outside of the publishing world, deserves a mention because it was the pioneer in ebook distribution services. Mark

Coker, the creator of Smashwords, came up with the brilliant idea to create one site to distribute a single book across all the other retailers. They negotiated a contract with the other retailers so you can upload your book on Smashwords and they will upload it to the other sites. The sole exception is Amazon, because they're *Amazon*. The formatting can be tricky, but in the end, you only need to manage uploading books to Amazon and Smashwords to reach every market in the world. The next thing you know, you're global.

Draft2Digital and BookBaby have the same model. Both require a small fee to use their site, but their sites have features that Smashwords lacks. They came after, so in certain respects, they improved on the model created by Smashwords. If you are interested in going wide release over Amazon exclusive, definitely check out these three retailers.

Other Retailers.

Ben here: So far, we've talked a lot about ebooks and their outlets. While they are likely to be the primary source of income for you, other avenues can have an enormous impact on your overall business.

As an indie author, you can get your books in the print and audio markets, virtually for free. It might be easier for you to consider each of these markets as a side business. Each requires its own learning curve and has its own benefits and drawbacks. Don't rush to expand until you are ready, but certainly include them in your plan.

Print. Getting a book in print is surprisingly simple, and it requires a minimal up-front investment. But to explain this, we first need to define POD publishing. POD stands for "Print on Demand." This indicates a book is printed after it is ordered. Companies like Random House save on the cost of books by ordering in bulk, but the costs go up for shipping, warehousing, and more shipping. POD allows indie authors to operate without an inventory because the book is printed and shipped by the retailer.

There are several POD publishers, but there are only two that I think are best. CreateSpace, owned by Amazon, is the first (and Honorée's favorite), while Lightning Source is the second.

CreateSpace. This POD company makes it easy and includes a step-by-step guide that will walk you through the process. They charge more for the books, so if you're planning on buying in bulk, you may want to consider the second option. However, CreateSpace can get your book into most print catalogs, including libraries. They will provide you with a free ISBN; however, we advise you to acquire your own ISBNs, and we'll discuss them more later.

Lightning Source. The second POD option is more complicated. It requires you to understand more about ISBNs, print runs, page length, cover dimensions, bleed effects, and so on. I'd only recommend this for experienced writers or writers who will be selling a lot of print books.

Audiobooks. Audiobooks are the fastest-growing market in the publishing world. Instead of buying books on CD, most listeners now download their books from sites like Audible or iTunes, purchasing and listening like they would to music. Audible, owned by Amazon, has direct links to Amazon, allowing a potential purchaser to navigate between the two sites. You can even get a discount on the audiobook if you own the ebook through a program called "Whispersync."

As an indie author, you have two methods of getting your book into audio. The first is to work directly with a producer, a perfectly viable option if a bit difficult. The second is through a subsidiary of Audible, a site called ACX.

Working with a producing company is an option that can't necessarily happen for everyone. Some audio firms will let you pitch your work to them. Others are invite-only. Audible has their own in-house production company, and they are always looking at their charts trying to see what authors deserve an invite. If you are invited, treat it like you would a traditional publishing offer, with caution and enthusiasm. Do your due diligence, weigh all your options, and make the decision that makes sense for you.

ACX is a site dedicated to pairing authors with narrators. You can post a sample of your work and narrators can record the sample. You then choose which narrator fits your needs best. My audio producer called this decision a $100,000 choice, and I agree. Don't just choose someone who sounds good. Look at the reviews of books your top choices have narrated until you can gauge the audience that follows them.

An important aspect of ACX is the method of payment. If your resources are limited, you can choose a royalty share option, where you and the narrator split the royalties. The second option is for you to pay the narrator outright, and you keep 100% of the royalties. This method can get pricey, with some of the better narrators charging a great deal for their time. In the long run, however, this investment can yield an impressive return.

Honorée here: If you can pay upfront for a narrator, we advise you to do so. You'll own the audio files outright and can upload, distribute, and sell them in any way you'd like. For most new authors, a royalty split is a good option because it allows you to engage a professional narrator without the substantial upfront costs. The narrator produces the audio files from your manuscript, and you split the royalties for the first seven years. This is a terrific option for beginning or even advanced authors because readers are consuming audio content in larger numbers than ever before—and the audience is growing as people learn how easy it is to listen to their favorite reads.

FORMATTING

No section on indie publishing would be complete without information on the importance of good book formatting. Nothing shouts "Amateur!" like a book that isn't formatted correctly. For the record, I hate formatting. It's tedious, frustrating, and, at times, mind-numbingly dull. I formatted my first book because I wanted to learn how, and I'm grateful I did. I spent days figuring out my first book, but now I do the same work in about two hours, a vast improvement. Knowing how to format also changes the way I write, because I know how it will be formatted in the final draft. Let's dive right in, shall we?

Table of Contents.

Ben here: Most digital retailers support a live table of contents. This means that you can use the Insert tab in Microsoft Word to create a table of contents for your book that will be clickable. On a tablet, readers can tap and go to whatever chapter they would like. This is great for readers and well liked. Even better, it makes your book look very professional. You can find an extensive section on this in the *Smashwords Style Guide*, a detailed book that answers many formatting questions.

Once you have a live table of contents, you may want to consider backlinks. Although the table of contents is live (meaning someone can click on the chapter and the ebook will go directly to it), the chapter headings are not. To add this, you have to go to each chapter heading, highlight, and then insert a hyperlink to the table of contents at the head of the book. This allows readers to click from a chapter back to the table of contents.

Pro Tip: The *Smashwords Style Guide* suggests placing a bookmark on the table of contents page linking you to the chapter headings. This is an excellent tool, but do not title the bookmark TOC (for table of contents). If you ever do a boxed set for your books, you'll end up with the same bookmark for all three books (because they are all named TOC), and you'll have to redo them. My suggestion is to title the top bookmark BookTitle_TOC (you can't have spaces). This way, whenever you box your book with another, the table of contents won't accidentally merge.

Images.

Amazon takes a small portion of the royalty as a download charge, and the larger the book, the higher the fee. If your book has lots of images, it's going to cost you in the long run. Print books have more flexibility, but the formatting can still be tricky. If you plan on having ornate scrollwork or images at the top of every chapter, it's going to drastically increase the formatting time. And if you do it wrong, it will take more time to correct. As you decide on the interior formatting, consider your intended impact. Will you sell more books with a beautiful interior? Maybe yes. Is it worth it? Maybe not.

Honorée here: It is also important to weigh whether those images add substantive value to your book. Sometimes a picture truly is worth a thousand words!

Honorée makes an excellent point. Don't delete them just because it will cost a few cents. The images may end up driving more sales!

If you don't have any desire to learn the formatting for yourself, you can hire a professional formatter to do the job for you. There are many freelance formatters that frequent author groups both online and in person. Ask around in indie author groups, and you are bound to find one. Expect the formatting to run $100–$1,500 depending on the length, content, and complexity of the book. If it's extremely complex, and you have a lot of headings, bullet points, or images, your investment will be higher.

Custom formatting will cost more, but your book will look *amazing*. Consider carefully if ornate, beautiful images or special fonts are going to help you achieve your goals and be consistent with your brand.

Honorée here: I cannot stress enough the importance of great formatting. If your text isn't fully justified, has odd line breaks, or is hard to read in any way, that is going to be a black mark against your book (and the reader may opt out of reading it now and forever). I wouldn't format my own books for any amount of money, so my preferred formatter is the team at 3CsBooks.com. They provide custom formatting, and they have experience formatting graphics, charts, and images in both print and digital files.

Also, an experienced formatter can make bulleted lists and images appear clean and even beautiful on your pages, print or digital. Your book never gets a second chance to make a first impression, and if a reader has a hard time reading your book, chances are they'll return it and find another read.

Amazon

Ben here: We'll spend the rest of this chapter on Amazon. Regardless of your personal feelings toward the company, Amazon is essential to book publishing. Nearly all authors earn more from Amazon than all other retailers combined. But before we get to the benefits, let's talk about one of the problems.

Piracy.

Copyright in the United States is owned at the point of creation and endures until seventy (70) years after the creator's death. Then it becomes public domain. Copyright aside, the unfortunate truth is that piracy in the world of publishing is a possibility.

The most common example is when a book gets copied and uploaded to pirated sites. Some argue that piracy increases your readership because those readers would never buy your book anyway. But they might talk to real buyers about your book, leading to more sales.

If you do decide to fight piracy, you'll need what's called a DMCA notice. You can easily find examples with a quick Google search. When you hear of a pirate site and check it for your books, send them a message with links to your titles and the DMCA notice.

Reviews and Your Advanced Reader Team

Honorée here: Reviews provide third-party validation for your book—a review (positive or negative) says someone has taken the time to read your book and share their opinion. It can be difficult to get reviews, so you must have a plan! Starting with your Advanced Reader Team (ART), and ending, well, never (just like your marketing), you should be looking for authentic reviews from the day you launch your book.

Your goal is to get as many reviews as possible, as quickly as possible. Of course, we all want five-star reviews that reinforce we are *the most awesome author who has ever lived, and our book is the most incredible book ever written.* (Good luck!) However, you're going to get one-star reviews that say you should *never* have written a book, followed by a five-star review saying your book is amazing. Not every book will be loved by everyone, but your book will be loved by many. Remember: the goal is to accumulate reviews!

Form an ART to launch with multiple reviews.

Your ART will help you publish your book with multiple reviews on your official launch day. I have an ART that consists of almost two hundred; however, these are folks who have asked to read *any* book I write. Your goal is to form an ART that consists of the ideal reader for your book.

Why? Because you want reviews from ideal readers so the online retailers can market your book to others who are likely to buy and read your books!

Here's how to build your ART:

1. **Recruit.** Send a note to your main email list and ask them to join your ART, and you can even start a Facebook group just for your ART. I gave mine a spiffy name: The Review Crew. Create an opt-in page through your email list provider. Make sure you let them know that in exchange for receiving a *free* advance copy of your book, they

are asked to provide an honest review on Amazon and Goodreads. During your soft launch (the day your book goes live, which is three to four days before the publicized date of your book launch), you could price the book at $0.99 specifically so that your ART can purchase it (more on that later). Be sure to review Amazon's policies where reviews are concerned, so you don't run afoul and end up having them deleted or worse (end up in Amazon jail).

Your ART gets their advance review copy two to three weeks prior to the launch. The more time you give them, the better chance they will have read the book prior to your launch day and have their review ready to go. I send a survey for them to fill out, complete with a space to write their review (this is important, see below).

2. **Send updates.** When they join, send them a couple of updates letting them know the book is almost ready and they'll have it on "Saturday the 14th" so they can start reading. If you give them an anticipated date, you'll find they are ready to begin reading because they expect it and make room on their calendars for it.

3. **Send the book.** Two to three weeks before the official launch, send your ART an advance review copy. You'll want PDF, .mobi (for Amazon Kindle), and .epub (for the iPad and all other digital readers). I use BookFunnel (http://bookfunnel.com) to deliver my advance copies for a couple of reasons: it isn't expensive

and has several options for use. Some people are truly tech savvy and know how to sideload a book onto their favorite electronic device. Others find this challenging. Make your life and your ART's life easy by providing them with a simple solution. Remember, the confused mind says no.

4. **Ask them to read it as soon as possible.** From one author to another, you've got to stay on top of your ART. Send them the book and expect them to, of their own accord and with no reminder, read the book and leave a review, you will most likely be sadly disappointed. Even the most responsible and organized people get distracted by everything from a new project to a kitten video.

   You can send emails or even video messages every couple of days. Feel free to provide content, bonuses, and extras that didn't make it into the book. The idea is to stay in pretty close touch over the three weeks prior to the launch.

   Plan to send a reminder to your entire ART every few days prior to the launch. Your ART is a group of your friends, family, and fans so be your authentic self in your videos and emails.

5. **Capture the best of the book.** If you started a Facebook group, or even a thread on your author page, have a separate thread asking the members to leave their favorite quotes and ideas there. You can do this by asking a question, or post one of

your favorite parts of the book, and ask them to do the same.

What you're going for with regular posts is group engagement. The more people post in the group, the more often each member of the ART will get notifications that serve as a reminder to read, buy, and review the book. Trust me; this works wonders.

6. **Social media magic.** Turn the best quotes into shareable social media graphics. I use the app WordSwag to turn photos and quotes into shareable posts. While someone might entirely miss words, a picture will grab their attention. Combined with a memorable quote, your photo can be liked and shared over and over.

7. **Continue to cultivate your ART.** Here's a complete list of action steps:

   a. Post (daily) videos (if you're using Facebook).

   b. Send those videos by email to the list.

   c. Give resources to share.

   d. Start threads at least once a day.

   e. Give encouragement, celebrate special moments, and be positive whenever you can.

   f. Make it easy for them to share your message by providing tweets and photo posts.

   g. Ask them to change their FB photo to a square graphic of your book for the day (it will show up on their timeline, and all their contacts will see it). You'll need a 2400 x 2400 pixel square version of your book cover for this, which your graphic designer can easily provide (you'll need it if you do an audio version of your book as well).

Exponential exposure is what you're after here. You never know when someone will see your graphic and take action by reading your book or hiring you.

8. **Launch.** As you build up to the launch day, provide ongoing cheerleading, but also give as much value as you possibly can. Yes, your ART has received a free copy of your book, and that's great; however, they've given you hours of their time by reading it. That's a W in the win column for you, without question. So, ask yourself what else you can provide, and do more than they can possibly expect. You'll find that they will do more than you expect.

Turn the launch into an event: a book launch party on Facebook. This event is completely separate from the pre-launch group. Invite your ART as well as *all* your other contacts to the event. Ask them to stop by on the day of your launch to say a few words, post pictures of themselves with your book, or share their favorite paragraph or quote. Give away prizes throughout the day. You could give away something you charge a lot for (such as a course, some consulting, or some swag). I've given away a coaching session, a copy of a different book, Starbucks gift cards, and even some "Cult of Honorée" merch.

Pro Tip #1: Dropping your book's price to $0.99 will increase the likelihood your advanced readers will purchase the book. Their reviews will then be *verified reviews*, which hold more weight with online retailers (specifically Amazon and iBooks). Having one hundred reviews gives you access to the "promised land" (where you get more organic promotion), and if many of them are verified, all the better.

Pro Tip #2: Unless your best friend, mom, or Aunt Sheila is *also* your ideal reader, tell them thanks but no thanks when they offer to buy and review your book.

When someone sends you an email or posts on social media they love your book, thank them profusely and ask them to leave a review.

I've started asking any three- or four-star reviewer what my book needed to deserve a five-star review (if I'm connected to them). Sometimes they answer, sometimes they don't. Some people just don't give five stars. Some people will write a bad review because they are jealous of your success. Again, it's the review that matters, not how many stars!

Ben here: The review system on almost any retail platform has benefits and drawbacks. One-star reviews carry a lot of weight, as do five-star reviews. Some authors have paid for positive reviews while others use the review system to push their perceived competitors down. We recommend you not attempt these practices because they hurt all authors! Amazon can and does delete reviews that seem fake, though their efforts are not always accurate. Many times, legitimate reviews are taken down with no notice or explanation. Those who do attempt fake reviews are more likely to have their reviews flagged as false. Imagine having fifty five-star reviews one day and the next they are gone. Don't pay for or elicit fake reviews because it can come back to bite you.

One-star reviews are also a reality, and sometimes they are given for odd reasons. Readers may rate a book one star because they dislike a character or the advice given in the book when the book is truly a solid five-star book. It can be frustrating to work so hard to release an incredible book only to have a reader give you a one-star review for inexplicable reasons. Also, avoid responding to bad reviews. Doing so can incite the reviewer to anger and increase the negativity around your book.

We don't want to scare you; we want to inform you. The publishing world has its share of problems like any other industry, and it's pointless to blame Amazon, the scammers, or any other company. You don't have control over them. You have control over you. If you are so inclined, you can get vocal on these issues (which we do not recommend), or you can simply navigate around them in your career (*this* is what we recommend—stay focused on building your book business, not complaining about anything over which you have no control). Either way, to master the market, you have to know the market. Now for the good news, and it's only fitting we match the cons, so the following are the best things about publishing on Amazon.

Author Central.

Honorée here: We talked about KDP as the platform for your books, and Author Central is the mini-platform within KDP for you to market yourself and your books. From this site, you can upload your author photo, your bio, and even link to your blog. This allows you to post on your blog and have the post show up on Amazon. That's a big deal. For anyone browsing content, they could find you and like what you are posting, and ultimately become a fan because they like your posts. This makes your Amazon Author Page feel live and organic, allowing readers to connect with authors in an unprecedented way. Also, you can look at your book ranking and author ranking (more on ranking in a few paragraphs!), allowing you to see your books' history. This might not seem like much, but it will help you measure the impact of sales and promotions, and even book releases.

"Also-Boughts."

Go to the bottom of a book page on Amazon, and you'll see the heading "Those who bought this product also bought…" This list is affectionately called the "Also-Boughts" by most authors and is a fantastic tool. If fans of a certain author begin to cross over to you, their book will show up on your Also-Boughts, and your book will show up on theirs. The higher you climb, the more you show up, meaning you can gain a presence on the page of big name authors.

Ad Campaigns.

Amazon's marketing tools are many and varied. Through a tab on the dashboard of KDP, you can look at Ad Campaigns. This tool hasn't been around long, and authors are still figuring it out, but it allows you to run ads for your books that show up on specific pages. Think of this as Amazon's version of pay-per-click advertising. It's still new, but it has huge potential. Check out Brian Meeks' *Mastering Amazon Ads* for a masterclass in advertising on Amazon.

Ranking.

Your rank on Amazon is enormously important, and it can give you information on your books and every book you buy. Working your book's ranking is a big topic, so we've saved that for *Market Like a Boss*. For now, you just need to understand that the ranking on Amazon is a comparative ranking. For example: if your book is 10,000 in the Kindle store, it is selling better than two million other books and not as well as 9,999 books at that moment. The rankings change hourly, and your book can, and probably will, move up or down every hour! As you prepare to publish, understand that a higher ranking translates into more exposure (like on the Also-Boughts) and can put you onto the bestseller lists.

In-House Marketing.

Amazon may invite you to participate in their in-house marketing. There are several ways that Amazon will offer to help an author, but they usually only happen if your books are doing great. You could be invited to join a Kindle Daily Deal, a Kindle Monthly Deal, or even Prime Reading. Your book might even get invited to one of the higher profile pages, like the Movers and Shakers page.

My *You Must Write a Book* was featured as a Kindle Monthly Deal in July 2017 for $1.99 (the normal price of the book is $7.99). It sold seven times as many books as the month before and made double the revenue. The most important impact this type of promotion has on your books is to help it rise in the ranking and expose it to new readers. Because I have a decent-sized backlist, I know my other books have increased discoverability by those who bought *You Must Write a Book*. If you get invited by Amazon to do a promotion, by all means, say *yes!*

I agree with Honorée here: The potential exposure far outweighs any risk. All told, there are a lot of interesting benefits you can get if you start climbing the charts. I should note that the other sites, like the iBookstore, have versions of this as well.

Sales Dashboard.

The sales dashboard on Amazon has recently been revamped, showing a graph of all your sales and Kindle Unlimited page reads. The tool makes it very easy to track the effects of promotions, new releases, and book signings. You can go into minute detail and examine every book over an extended period, a tool both vital and satisfying.

KDP Select.

Other sites may have similar marketing programs, but KDP Select is all Amazon. The digital exclusivity may hurt, but the ability to run discount and free promotions on Amazon can be huge. I credit much of my first year's growth to a few free promotions on my first book. These tools are easy to use and learn and, with a little marketing, can be a game changer.

The Select program requires you to publish your ebook only on Amazon's KDP platform, and in return, you get certain promotional benefits. (You can still publish without using the Select program.) This topic will be covered in more depth in *Market Like a Boss* because it's a marketing decision. However, for the sake of this book, here are a few highlights.

1. It has a 90-day enrollment. It's easy to opt out, but for the duration, your book must be exclusive to Amazon in ebook form. (Print books can be elsewhere.)

2. Your book is included in Kindle Unlimited (KU for short), and this can be great for new authors or new series. Currently, authors get paid about half a penny per page read in the program. That might not sound like much, but I frequently earn more from my KU page reads than I do from my book sales. That's thousands of dollars a month!

3. It's worth doing your research. The choice to enroll in KDP Select is important, so read everything you can on its benefits and drawbacks.

A Note on DRM Software.

One of the boxes you fill out on Amazon asks if you want DRM software. DRM stands for Digital Rights Management, and it is intended to slow the advance of piracy. Some think it works; others think it fails utterly and only punishes the reader. If you don't have an opinion, you'll need one, and a quick Google search will help you find the answer.

I was initially reluctant to skip DRM software. After all, it's meant to stop piracy, right? However, I then read an article that compared the sales results of books on Amazon that used DRM against those that didn't. To my surprise, the books without DRM did better. I took the plunge and skipped it for my third series, and it did sell better. There is a myriad of factors that could have influenced it, but I've since skipped the DRM software.

A Note on Kindle Matchbook.

Another little box you have the option to check when you set up your books in KDP references the Kindle Matchbook program. This program allows someone to get a discount on the ebook if they have already purchased the print version.

Many people love having a print copy and the option to purchase the digital version for just a little bit more.

PUBLISH LIKE A BOSS

Depending on the price of your paperback and print books, you can let them either have the digital version for free or purchase it for $0.99, $1.99, or $2.99. We advise making the second purchase a "no-brainer" by pricing it just right and in alignment with the prices of your book. If you're uncertain as to what is just right, look at comparable titles in your genre. If you are higher than they are, it will discourage sales; lower might encourage sales, but also give the impression the book is worth less than it truly is.

A Note on Previewing Your Book

When you go to upload your manuscript on Amazon, you will be able to view a digital proof. You can see exactly how your book is going to look on a tablet or smartphone. You can even look through every page up close if you would like. This handy tool is incredibly useful, and I recommend you use it with every publication on Amazon.

CATEGORIES AND KEYWORDS

Honorée here: While categories and keywords are topics that are addressed in more depth in *Market Like a Boss*, you'll need to have at least a basic knowledge when you're first publishing your book.

Let's start with categories.

When you're setting up your book in the backend of your chosen online retailers, you will initially choose two main categories for your book. For this example, we'll follow how Amazon works. To select your first category, you will select from a short list of possibilities. If you're writing a business book, most probably you'll choose *Nonfiction: Business*. If your book is in a specialty area, you'll likely find a separate category to choose, such as *Nonfiction: Business & Economics: Business Law* or *Nonfiction: Business & Economics: Personal Success*.

Ben here: The fiction categories work the same way, but the challenge is that the categories you see on the Amazon shopping page may not show up on the KDP dashboard. You'll need to cross reference to search for the best genre that fits your needs. The keywords you choose can push your book into other categories unintentionally. (I know, it's confusing.) Don't stress too much, though, you can change the categories at any time post-publication. Go with what seems to fit best, and you should be fine.

Honorée here: It is easy to become dismayed because while the categories might seem obvious, these main categories have several (perhaps hundreds) of popular books that are selling well and taking up valuable space on the bestseller charts. In other words, how are you going to get your book noticed by both the online retailer (so they will promote it to other logical buyers) as well as prospective readers as they scan for their next read?

The trick is to identify subcategories where your prospective readers might find themselves searching for the perfect read and set that as your second category. For example, *Publish Like a Boss* is a reference book on writing. We want to find as many readers as possible, so we identify the main category, *Reference*, then the logical subcategory, *Writing, Research & Publishing Guides*.

Let's take a closer look at this category. The main question we ask ourselves is, *What are my chances of dominating this category?* The number one book in the category *Writing, Research & Publishing Guides* is ranked 1,127 in the overall Amazon store, which is a fantastic rank! This book, *Turn Your Computer into a Money Machine*, is selling a couple of dozen copies every day and has remained a bestselling book since its release in November 2015. With consistent sales and more than 450 great reviews, this book stands to continue to sell well.

But all is not lost—let's check to see how well the one hundredth book is selling to determine if this is a good category for our book. The one hundredth book is ranked 32,475. Not stellar, but still selling at least a few copies a day, making it tough for a new book to find readers because most people don't scroll past the top twenty. To crack into that category would take some work!

We are better off identifying a subcategory we can rank well in from the get-go. As our book gains in popularity, we can try to work our way up the charts in the next category up. For now, there are fourteen subcategories, and our book could do well in several of them (*fiction, genre fiction, nonfiction, publishing & books,* or *writing skills*). By the time you read this, we will have analyzed which categories we can rank well in and will ask to be placed in those categories.

Ben here: My personal favorite is to find a top 100 list with room for growth like Honorée suggested, and pair it with a harder-to-reach category. One of my chosen categories regularly has a ranking range of 50 for the first book to 4,000 for the one-hundredth book. The second category on the same book has 50 for the first book and 60,000 for the one-hundredth. This means that it's easier to rank high on the lesser-selling list, giving the book some exposure, while hitting the hotter list with promotions and marketing. Again, you should feel free to change your categories a little or a lot!

Requesting Amazon to put your book into a specific category is simple:

- Log in to your online retailer dashboard.

- Click on *Help*, then *Contact Us*.

- Choose *Book Details*, then *Categories and Keywords*.

- Enter your book's title and ASIN, then list the desired category.

- Within 24-48 hours, you'll receive an email that your book has been added to the requested category, and you'll be able to see the change.

Pro Tip: Copy and paste the EXACT keyword string you find on other books like yours. This makes it easier for KDP to update your book's category.

Putting your book in the correct categories will help drive sales because potential readers go looking for new books or other books on subjects they are interested in (or, in the case of fiction, genres they love to read). Make it easy for readers to find your book by putting its cover right next to other books they may have read. Also, online retailers (Amazon specifically) will market your book to readers who have read similar books, so taking the time to research the proper categories is key.

Now, on to keywords.

Honorée here: Keywords are an *enormous* topic. We could spend fifty pages discussing how keywords could be optimized and the level of detail in finding the perfect keyword. Because it has such a bearing on your marketing efforts, it gets more attention into *Market Like a Boss*. However, since you need them in publishing, we're going to touch on them here as well.

Search keywords help readers find your book when they browse online. You can enter keywords or short phrases that describe your book and are relevant to its content. The best keywords are those that do not repeat words in the title, category, or description, as these are already used to help readers find your book. Some types of keywords are prohibited and can result in the removal of content. For example, you can't have profanity or the title of another book as a keyword.

It bears repeating that keywords can be short phrases—a series of words that describe your book. Most people wouldn't just put "dating" in the search bar; they would search for books on "dating for people over fifty." Those seven words would be considered a keyword phrase. Make sense?

To find keywords people are searching for, I use a tool called KDP Rocket, which is great for books not only on Amazon but also other online retailers that request keywords.

How Do I Choose a Title and Subtitle?

Perhaps one of the most important decisions you'll make is the title of your book. The title is *the topic* of the book; the subtitle is the *promise.* In other words, your title conveys what the book is about, and the subtitle tells what the reader will get in exchange for reading the book.

Here are four boxes to check when creating your title and subtitle:

- ☐ Be brief. You can eliminate "how to" (that's implied in nonfiction) from your title, along with any unnecessary words.

- ☐ Be specific. Identify your book's topic in simple language, targeting your ideal readers by using words they already know and would use to find your book.

- ☐ Be direct and descriptive. Tell readers exactly what the book is about. (Don't make them guess because they won't!)

- ☐ Include any pertinent positioning (if your book is longer, shorter, based in science, has an edge).

Settling on a title can take time—feel free to take the necessary time because there's no need to rush. As I mentioned, I redid my first book, including the title, because it was awful! If your book doesn't sell and you know you've done everything you possibly could, it might need a title change (and there's no harm in that)!

For fiction, you need to be careful with the subtitle. It can easily bog down a fiction reader, and they will lose interest before purchasing your book. Fiction books work best when the title is clear and pairs well with the cover content. Great titles can connect with readers, so don't get too attached to any title until you've done your homework. Also, keep in mind that a fiction book is typically part of a series, which for many fiction writers acts as the subtitle.

On a final note, when working on your book, it is best to ask for advice and input only from those who can help. Your friends, family, and coworkers are not in this group. While some folks advise you to do what's called A/B testing with your covers or titles, polling your friends on Facebook or asking for input from your closest friends (unless they are also bestselling authors *in your genre*) is a fool's errand.

You'll compound the error of creating your own cover by asking your friends on Facebook if they like blue, black, or red font. They simply *don't know*, so unveil your finished work only after it has gone through the proper production.

Great point, Honorée. Asking your friends for advice on the font options would be like me asking an accountant which car engine he likes most. The highest-quality advice comes from two sources: those in the business who know, and that genre's readers. Everyone else will skew your results and ultimately weaken your brand.

How Much Should I Charge for My Book?

Honorée here: Identifying the best price for a fiction book can be difficult. You might think it's worth $8.99 for the Kindle edition, just like the traditional publishers charge. But it's best to enter this conversation with the right perspective. Your readers—not you—determine the perceived value of your book.

If your book is twice the length of everything in the genre, you might think you can charge double. Unfortunately, doing so means you will sell less. Readers in a genre have an expectation that a certain book of a certain genre is worth a certain amount. Don't fight them on it, because they're going to win. We want you to win, too, because they purchase your book!

Your brand also impacts the price. If you are a reputable, well-known author, you might want to raise your prices a little. The number of reviews, the quality of the work, etc., all impact the perceived value.

I usually recommend for authors to look at books in their genre. Compare your book to those with the same length and publication avenue. Generally, a full-length, indie-published book sells for between $2.99 and $4.99.

Pricing your nonfiction book is a combination of your brand, your expertise, the problem the book solves, and the market. If you price it too high, people won't buy it. If you price it too low, you may not get the right buyers. Also, when I buy a book at a lower price (like

$0.99 or $1.99), I have less urgency to read it, and the perceived value is low. The goal is to price the book at just the right price so it will sell and be read *as soon as possible.*

One thing I want to address quickly is the fact that some newer authors have a hard time selling "all" of their knowledge for less than $10. I understand how you feel, but let me say this: first, you aren't giving away everything you know (it just isn't possible!), and second, you must keep in mind your desired outcome for the book. If you're using your book as your business card or to sell products, ultimately, you're not looking for the $5 you'll make from the book; you're potentially looking for the thousands or tens of thousands of dollars you'll make from your fees.

Let's start with the good news (and this time, it is all good news!): people are willing to pay more for a book that solves a problem. And the bigger the problem, the more they'll pay. If your book helps the reader avoid pain, gain pleasure, or both, people will gladly pay!

If you are a recognized expert, readers will pay more for your book because they know spending even five minutes with you would cost them multiple times the book's price.

I would price a nonfiction ebook no less than $2.99 (unless you are running a promotion), and the price increases from there commensurate with these other factors:

- The length of the book. The closer you get to 250 or 300 pages, the closer you get to $9.99. If you are unknown, however, consider pricing the book a few dollars less to get those first few thousand critical sales. If your book is short yet packs a punch, don't be afraid to price it at $3.99 or $4.99.

- The strength of your brand. If you are well-known, have a high-quality brand, or you command top-shelf fees for your time, you can charge between $7.99 and $9.99.

- Your status as an expert. If you are *the expert* (or at least one of a dozen or less) in your field, you can price on the higher side.

- Your renown. Even if you know your stuff, if others don't know your name (and your bio won't knock their socks off), avoid charging more than $7.99 (I'd stick with $4.99–$6.99).

Keep in mind you want your potential reader to be excited to buy and read your book—so make your price a "no-brainer." You want your reader to think, "*Of course* I'll pay $6.99 to learn three steps to protect my assets!" Or, "*I can't wait* to pay $9.99 to learn the ten things I need to know to make a million dollars in the next thirty days!"

Regarding your print edition, I generally add not less than $6 and not more than $10 to the ebook edition price (depending upon page count and the factors listed above).

One last note on pricing: you can always adjust your price up or down. *If Divorce is a Game, These are the Rules* was originally priced at $4.99. I raised the price to $7.99, and sales went up. Then, when I released *The Divorced Phoenix*, I lowered the price of the book to $3.99. Now both books are priced where they each sell a dozen copies a month, even without my constant promotion.

3

PUBLISH FICTION LIKE A BOSS

Ben here: Fiction is an entirely different beast than nonfiction, meaning that if you truly want to write both, you've got your work cut out for you. This year marks my first foray into writing and publishing nonfiction, but not the first time I've considered the prospect. I didn't have the time or the resources to dive into and master the differences between the two genres. But when Honorée and I discussed working together, I jumped at the chance. She knows far more than I do about nonfiction, so I'll focus on what I know best: the fiction. Let's start with the most significant question you might have.

Fiction: What Sells?

Unfortunately, this question has a tricky answer. First, you should look at several other topics. The fiction world is broken up into markets (nonfiction is, too, and Honorée will talk about that in the next chapter). Large markets include Romance. Smaller markets such as Coming of Age Fantasy. Niche markets might have less than two hundred books, while large markets have hundreds of thousands. This creates an interesting dynamic. Smaller markets allow authors to gain exposure a bit easier because there is little competition. Larger markets are tougher—it's hard to compete against so much volume. Think of it like opening a new restaurant in a tiny rural community versus in New York City. Your restaurant would probably be popular in the rural community, but your population of interested patrons would be limited. New York, on the other hand, has virtually no limit on diners, but getting them to come to your restaurant is extremely difficult. Is one better than the other? Not necessarily. It depends on what you want out of your career.

Romance is the largest market, with reported sales of twice those of the second largest market. The second largest is a tie between suspense/thriller and nonfiction, and third is fantasy and science fiction. If you want to look closer at these numbers, go to the Author Earnings Report. The report also shows which publication avenue has the largest market share of each genre.

Each genre has many smaller markets of varying sizes. If you want to know the number of books in a given category, simply navigate through the Amazon departments and look to the top left, where you'll see the total number of books. From there you can see if the genre is selling well based on the sales rank of the top ten books listed.

Part of publishing is deciding where your book has the best chance of connecting with an audience. Do your homework and research the categories on any platform you plan on using. If you don't know where your book fits because it's multi-genre, that's okay. But you'll still have to know the category you want to select. Again, browse the existing categories for ideas.

Pro Tip: The categories listed on the KDP dashboard are different than the ones on Amazon. If you don't see the one you want on KDP, but you do see it on Amazon, then it requires keywords to get your book listed in that specific category. Or you can e-mail KDP and give them the exact category you want for your book, and they can help you.

SHOULD I WRITE A SERIES OR SINGLE TITLES?

Writing a series versus single titles has a clear winner, and this is mostly due to the nature of ebooks. In the past, readers of print novels were required to go and seek other books by the writer. Perhaps they went to the library or bookstore or talked to a friend. Now many readers are using ebooks, and when they finish, book two is just a click away. (Don't forget your live links!) A series of books is connected, and readers tend to naturally continue through the series. You'll have a drop from each book, but ultimately, you have a built-in audience that is already moving on to the rest of your books.

A reader of a single title may enjoy the book immensely but may not ever seek out other books by the author. Even with live links, the reader finishes the book and is likely happy with your ending. There is no drive to continue to the next in the series.

However, as powerful as writing a series can be, it has two major drawbacks. If you write a series of twenty books, it can deter new readers from starting the series. They're hesitant about committing to such a large work. The second major disadvantage is that regardless of the size of the series, you can only really market the first in that series (and maybe the boxed set if you have one), limiting your marketing options.

Pro Tip: Make sure the first of your series is a powerhouse. It must command attention because the bulk of your marketing will fall on its shoulders. If sales of your series seem to have stagnated, consider revamping the covers, especially the cover of the first book. A new cover can do wonders for an old series.

Single titles have the opposite benefit. Each book can be marketed separately, making it possible to have numerous promotions running simultaneously. And although readers might not flock to other books you have written, a portion will jump to your other titles.

How Long Should My Book Be?

This is a common question that again has a complicated answer. Genre fiction, like fantasy and science fiction, favors longer content. In the 100,000 words realm. (Oh, and just so you know, publishing is based on word count, not page count.) Romance typically prefers shorter content, around 60,000 to 80,000 words. Suspense and thriller fall between the two. These numbers are just averages, not ideals. Your excellent romance novel might be 120,000 words; however, in that case, you might consider splitting one book into two.

Shorter fiction is another matter entirely. Serialized short stories can be anywhere from 5,000 to 40,000 words and are present in any genre. Many successful indie writers have written a short story series and then lumped them into a boxed set for marketing purposes. In serialized fiction, embedded links are even more important.

An important note about the choice of genre is your brand. We'll talk a lot about branding in *Market Like a Boss* and later in this book. But for now, you want to understand what brand you wish to grow. That's because a consistent brand gains momentum. As of this moment, I'm eighteen books into the forty I want to write in my fantasy world. That's thirteen years writing in the same world. My readers know what to expect from me, and my fans continue to return. If you love to write many things at once, just be prepared for an uphill climb, because readers won't necessarily like all the genres you choose to publish in. Consistency in your publication schedule can be tremendously powerful. Which brings me to the next topic...

WHEN SHOULD I PUBLISH?

Great question. (I know I'm asking the questions and then answering them, but that way I always know the answer!) The timing of your publication can play a big hand in how well your books perform. Romance books are frequently released around Valentine's Day, while children's books do better during the school year. The entire publishing world sells less over the summer. The important thing about your publication schedule is that it builds.

Publishing fiction is all about momentum—especially in a series. This is due to the boost you get when a book is released. On nearly every platform, you gain increased exposure because the book is new. Amazon's boost lasts thirty days and, to a lesser extent, ninety days. Beyond that, your book is left to its own devices, and unless something keeps it relevant, it will gradually be pushed down in the rankings by newer releases.

Momentum is built using the system to consistently maintain exposure. Let's say you want to write a trilogy. If you release one book per year for three years, you would likely build and then lose momentum each year, making it very difficult to capture an audience. Whatever readership you gain will likely move on with too much time in between books, and you will have to capture them again.

On the flip side, let's say you write the trilogy over three years and release them all one week apart. On the plus side, you would get a lot of exposure quickly because you'd have three new products, but the total time you'd be on a list is less than two months. On top of that, you will be limiting how many can purchase book one before book two is released.

Both options have major challenges. I recommend a place between these two extremes. My personal preference is to release books in a trilogy three months apart. I typically release one in midsummer, one in September, and one in December. I write three books a year and could release them four months apart, but I condense it to three. This is what works for me. It may be the exact opposite of what works for you. If you write short fiction, I recommend a much smaller publication schedule. What matters is that you explore and find what works for you.

Christmas has an interesting dynamic and deserves a separate mention. We all know that sales spike over the holidays, but how about books? Well, here's where it gets complicated. Reports indicate that book sales spike as well, likely because readers are traveling and getting new, empty Kindles that need to be filled. However, these buyers frequent the bestsellers, meaning books lower than a certain threshold sell worse over the holidays. Unless you can top 20,000 in the rankings, odds are the holidays will push your books downward. This means you have a choice. Either build your momentum to cross that threshold, or try to gain momentum at a different time during the year.

The day of the month and week can matter as well. Lots of larger publishers release on the first of the month, so purchasing tends to favor that time. Days of the week vary by genre; religious books, for example, do better on Sunday. Consider your genre and study the results before you plan your publication schedule.

Pro Tip: If you want to hit a major bestseller list, keep in mind what day they start recording sales. *The New York Times*, for example, starts on Sunday and ends Saturday.

4

PUBLISH NONFICTION LIKE A BOSS

Honorée here: Writing and publishing a nonfiction book can be beneficial for scores of reasons. It can add to your credibility, help you increase your fees, and expand your brand. You can make money from the direct sales of your book. You can earn more money by using your book to engage more clients or customers. Or both.

The fastest and best way to establish your authority is to have a book with your name on the front. And let's face it: authors are *cool*. (Insert smile here.) Seriously, when someone asks what I do for a living, and I say, "I write books," they want to know more.

I'm psyched about this section because I get to share everything I wish I'd known when I first started publishing books: what to consider when writing a book; when and how to publish professionally (ahem, *like a boss*); whether to write a standalone, a series, or several complimentary books; and how to strategically publish to monetize your book in multiple ways. And these are just the tip of the iceberg.

I've now written almost a dozen books for writers, all of them completely by accident. When I attended the predecessor to the Smarter Artist Summit in Austin, Texas, in 2014, I was inspired to write *Prosperity for Writers*. That series is now five books strong with a sixth on the way. I also penned *You Must Write a Book* and the companion guide *I Must Write My Book* to help professionals finally get their book written. I reference those books in this section so you can go deeper into a certain area of interest if you need to. If I didn't, this section would be longer than *The Iliad of Homer* and ain't nobody got time for that!

However, just so you don't think I'm failing to put what you need in this book just so you'll buy my other books (that would be rude)—if there's one of my other books you'd like to read in exchange for an honest review, just shoot me an email and I'll make it happen. I do think you'll find this section meaty enough to help you take your nonfiction game up several notches and truly publish each book you write from this day forward in a way that will serve you over the long term.

NONFICTION: WHAT SELLS?

What nonfiction books have the best sales? This question has a couple of answers.

The books that sell the best are those that meet one, some, or all of the following criteria:

- **Catchy titles**. *Think & Grow Rich* and *The Four-Hour Work Week* are two books with catchy titles—you remember them the first time you hear or see them. Who doesn't want to just "think and grow rich" or only work four hours a week (if only!)? The title of your book can make the difference between it languishing in obscurity or becoming a hit. Pam Grout originally published her runaway hit, *E-Squared: Nine Do-It-Yourself Energy Experiments That Prove Your Thoughts Create Your Reality*, under a different title: *God Doesn't Have Bad Hair Days*. The difference in the sales of these two books, which are virtually the same book, is startling! Pam knew her book was good and would change people's lives, but it just wasn't selling. It wasn't until she gave it a make-over—new cover and new title—that the book began to sell.

  Crafting your book's title with as much care as you would put into your business name can increase sales exponentially. Shortly, I'll share my formula for creating a *just right* title that sells.

- **Compelling messages**. *The Five-Second Rule* by Mel Robbins has become the book everyone is reading. Mel's simple rule is impacting lives in a major way, allowing space for people to act right now instead of putting it off indefinitely.

I imagine you won't write a book you don't think has a compelling message. Consider this: your message must be compelling to the reader in order for them to read it *now*, love it enough to leave a review, and share it with others. Books with compelling messages can also be books with polarizing messages. I advise you take a stand, whatever that stand is, and stand in your truth. The more compelling the message, the more the right readers will find your book, love it, and share it—making, ultimately, for great sales.

- **Reader connection**. *Chicken Soup for the Soul* started as a stand-alone title and became a major bestseller and cultural phenomenon. As of 2013, more than two hundred titles in the series had been published, with many more planned. The reason these books became a household name is because of the connection readers had with the stories. People won't be able to quote a paragraph from your book, but when you include stories, they may retell those stories to others as they convince them to read your book.

If you can write a book that connects on a deep level with your reader, you will find that your readers will go from being fans to *super* fans. And what do super fans do? They shout about your book from the rooftop (or in today's world, on Facebook and Twitter, and to their friends, family, colleagues, and neighbors).

- **Problem-solving**. People seek advice in three major categories: *money, sex*, and *weight loss*. If your book can solve a problem, especially in any of these three areas, you have a terrific shot at a successful book (however you define successful). *Rich Dad Poor Dad* by Robert T. Kiyosaki has over 6,000 reviews and ranks in the top 1,000 books on Amazon even today, eighteen years after its original publication as a self-published book. *The Four-Hour Body: An Uncommon Guide to Rapid Fat-Loss, Incredible Sex, and Becoming Superhuman* hits on the other two of the three major topics, so it is no surprise it has over 3,200 reviews and is in the top 5,000 books seven years after publication.

Nonfiction books that successfully solve a problem sell and sell and sell.

Your goal should be to truly solve the problem of your reader *even if* they don't ever hire you or buy anything else from you. Why? Because happy readers become fans, and fans will love your book and write a great review on Amazon. Reviews on Amazon give third-party validation that you know your stuff and I, the peruser, should *buy* your book and perhaps buy you.

Ben here: This point is so crucial! Readers can feel if your goal is to sell them on your business. They can also sense if your book is trying to solve their problem. Be genuine, and the readers will respond much better.

Honorée here: Your book can hit all four criteria, and you can have that runaway bestseller mentioned earlier—making you a bona fide bestselling author and your book a perennial bestseller.

The number one way readers find a book is through personal recommendation. I see it all the time on Facebook: *What are you reading? Who can give me a good book recommendation?* Readers are always looking and listening for their next great read.

Pro Tip: Do your best to write a book that has a catchy title, has a compelling message, connects deeply with the reader, and successfully solves a problem.

But those four criteria may not be enough. In fact, before you write your (first) book, there are a few other things to consider:

SHOULD I WRITE A SERIES, SINGLE TITLES, OR A GROUP OF COMPLEMENTARY BOOKS?

Allow me to explain. If you're reading this particular book, I would imagine you are, or intend to be, the author of multiple books. In fact, I imagine you as someone who would like *only* to write books, or use your book(s) to sell services like I do (such as consulting, coaching, and speaking) for a living. I mention this because it is imperative you apply the proper forethought to your book business.

Write a Single Title.

A single book is fine if it serves a solid or complementary purpose in your primary business. *Tall Order!* (2004 edition) started out as a single book. (I wasn't a writer, nor did I consider myself an author, remember? Mark Victor Hansen said, "You must write a book," and so I did.) I didn't know to look at my overall business and see how a book would fit in, add any strategy to my writing, or consider where I wanted to go in the future.

You absolutely can write one book, then turn it into a coaching program, a keynote presentation, a workshop, or even a course. The content of your book can be repurposed into multiple formats and therefore multiple streams of income.

However, you might want to do one or both of the following (depending on how many books you decide to write):

Write a Series.

Again with no forethought, I got the idea to write *The Successful Single Mom.* Almost immediately I had the idea to write several other books to create a series, but my coach at the time discouraged the idea, saying, "You won't make any money. There's no money in books."

Side note: ironically, I still hear that today—even though I've made seven figures multiple times over from my combined title sales. And I'm not alone. Lots of folks are writing books for a living. Go figure.

Anyway, I eventually decided (a) I wanted to write the series anyway and (b) I had nothing to lose and everything to gain. After discovering I had earned almost $10,000 in royalties I hadn't received due to an error (okay, it was due to my error and stupidity, but that's a story for another day), I was more excited than ever to get those books out into the world, helping single moms. *The Successful Single Mom* became a six-book series and is currently the bestselling book series for single moms. I have over 60,000 unique hits to my single mom blog every month, and countless women have written to me that one or more of the books helped them change their lives.

You might want to write one book containing "everything you know," only to discover your book is too complex or frankly too long for a reader to digest.

Enter: the option to write a series. I tackled each problem a single mom faces in each individual book. I covered the challenges I had faced and shared how I had gotten rich, fit, found love again, and cooked quick and healthy meals for my finicky eater. I even partnered with a co-author on *The Successful Single Mom Gets an Education* to help single moms go back to school (without getting taken advantage of or putting themselves in a debt hole they could never climb out of).

I also wrote *Prosperity for Writers* and then partnered with Brian Meeks to write three other books in the series. I'm currently working on the sixth book in that series because it is doing so well.

As Hal Elrod's business partner in *The Miracle Morning* book series, we started out with two books he already had in mind: *The Miracle Morning for Salespeople* and *The Miracle Morning for Network Marketers*. We're over a dozen into the series, and our experience has taught me a few things, such as choose your co-authors with care (make sure everyone has equally-sized platforms, morals, and work ethic), publish consistently, and focus on where you can make the most impact.

Whether you write a single book or a series, you'll want to choose your topic with care. Publishing regularly will boost your brand. Finally, a book that makes the most impact benefits everyone.

You can decide to write a book and see how it goes, or you can decide to write a series and simply start with one book. Check out the strategy section in *Market Like a Boss* for advice on how to launch the books in your series.

Write Complementary Books.

If you want your books to connect, you don't necessarily have to write a series. My books *Tall Order!*, *Vision to Reality*, and *Business Dating* are all books that address common challenges business folks have: getting and staying organized, turning the vision they have for their professional life into their real life, and networking effectively (respectively). You can read one, or you can read them all. The books complement each other and give my readers somewhere else to go when they like the book they have read. Each book is yet another place to get cost-effective advice that makes a difference and solves a problem.

I wouldn't put all three of those topics into one book, but all three topics could be important to a business person. I make sure each book mentions the others, and without going too much into what we cover in *Market Like a Boss*, I use each book to expand the awareness of my readers about other books I've written as well as my other products and services.

Pro Tip: Decide what you initially want out of your book(s) and book business, and be open to other possibilities.

How Long Should My Book Be?

Nonfiction books run between 30,000 and 70,000 words. Many short-and-sweet books sell, and many tomes (that could double as a museum door stop) sell. You'll want to keep in mind, however, that people are consuming their content digitally, in snippets of time, and are hard-pressed to find the time to read. I advocate for short books without a lot of fluff or filler.

Your book is your book, and you can make it as long or as short as you'd like. Your book can and should include everything want and need to say, nothing more and nothing less.

It's your book and you can do what you like. Isn't that fabulous? I think so!

Pro Tip: Make sure your book is at least one hundred physical pages (about 30,000 words, in a 5x8 format), so you can have the title of your book and your name on the spine.

WHEN SHOULD I PUBLISH?

There are several answers to this question.

Answer #1: When you've said everything you want to say. This answer is short and sweet: your book is done and ready to be published when you've included all of the advice, information, and inspiration needed.

But there are a few other things to consider as noted below, and they aren't as simple.

Answer #2: When you're able to publish professionally. In addition to writing a fantastic book, here are the five most important boxes to check to greatly increase (and even multiply) your chances of success:

You have a professional (and awesome) cover.

A great cover says, *look at me, buy me, I'm going to solve your problem!* A crappy cover does not get seen, or bought, or read. Your book is destined for obscurity, no matter how fabulous the content. A bad cover is one of the biggest reasons a book doesn't sell. Try 99Designs. com, ask us for one of our resources, or check out our resource section at the end of this book.

You've had at least one round of professional editing—maybe two, if it's your first go-around.

Typos, incorrect grammar, missing words—these create a bumpy ride for your reader. Additionally, readers expect a high standard when they pick up a book (and will put it down in disgust when a book does not meet their standard). *In addition to your cover, editing is the largest and perhaps the most important investment you will make in your book, and worth every penny.* Do I sound like a broken record? Good. Because I cannot stress enough how important great editing is! Hint: Don't use your neighbor who used to be an English teacher, or someone who "thinks they can edit," or your street team. Professional editors only!

Your sales copy and book description have been professionally crafted.

The description is the number one reason people buy a book. For around $300, you can get a top-shelf book description *that will sell your books.* The cover piques their interest; the book description copy converts their interest to a sale.

Your book's interior has been carefully and cleanly formatted.

In addition to editing, another way to ensure a smooth ride for your readers is to have a professional design the layout of your interior files. Your investment will be between $400 and $700 and will guarantee your ebook and paperback versions will look professional and read well. If you want customized designs, it'll cost extra, but I promise you it's worth every penny. I highly recommend 3CsBooks.com. The folks over there design all of my books (and my clients' books) beautifully. Also, because they are creating custom designs, the books don't look like every other book out there.

Ben here: When I first started, the interior layout of my book was not overly complicated. I didn't want drop caps, background artwork, multiple fonts, or complicated chapter headings. Because of this, I spent about a week learning how to format my books and that knowledge has saved me thousands of dollars.

Honorée here: There's a distinct parallel in this. If you want professional work, you can either pay with *cash* or pay with *time*. Either way, it's going to cost you. It just depends which resource is the one you wish to spend.

One caveat: regardless of your skill in editing, I still highly recommend getting a professional editor. It's about gaining their perspective as much as their skills. You can learn a lot, but you cannot learn to look at a book from someone else's perspective.

Your book has had a final proofread.

The final proofread is not part of the editing process. This last pass of your manuscript happens after each edit and review process is complete. The final proofread is an important piece of the puzzle. You'll have looked through your book so many times, your eyes will be crossed (and therefore you'll miss errors obvious to someone else).

It doesn't cost much to have a professional proofreader go through what you think is your final version and catch those pesky misspellings, missing words, and typos. Be sure to use a different person to proofread than the one who did your editing. At some point, we just can't see the errors that exist anymore, and a fresh set of eyes is crucial.

The idea of the five important components above is to create a professional product you'll be able to sell with pride! One that is enjoyable to read and that can withstand the scrutiny of your readers.

As more and more people self-publish and do so in a way that is virtually indistinguishable from the big publishers, you must make sure your publishing game is tight. You deserve it. Your book deserves it. Your readers deserve it. And finally, your book's success depends on it. When you've successfully completed these five critical steps, you can hit "publish" with complete confidence your book is ready for the world!

WHEN IS THE BEST TIME TO PUBLISH MY BOOKS?

As the cool kids say, *timing is everything.* The advice I give aspiring authors depends upon a few factors:

- **In conjunction with an event.** Do you have a summit, seminar, or convention where having your book would be helpful or even critical? Several of my clients have published in conjunction with an event, and I published *You Must Write a Book* to coincide with a media breakfast Amazon hosted in October 2016. If you have an event you host, attend, or speak at, you might consider publishing your book a week or so beforehand and announce it at the event.

- **In conjunction with a holiday or "National [Insert] Day."** *The Successful Single Mom* was released prior to Mother's Day so friends and family of single moms could give it as a gift. We released *The Miracle Morning for College Students* in May to coincide with high school graduations and *The Miracle Morning for College Students Companion Planner* in August, just as kids were getting ready for school.

I published each of my books on divorce around the time divorce filings tend to spike (January and June). If there is an apparent time of year it makes sense to publish, then target either the specific holiday or even a month ahead of time (so your book has gained some momentum by the official day).

If there's no obvious target date for your book, I advise choosing one of the following:

- - **The first quarter of the year.** The earlier you can publish in a calendar year, the longer your book will be "this year's book." Also, if you can publish your book on or close to the first Monday of the year, especially if it is self-improvement in nature, it can find the audience focused on their New Year's Resolutions.

- **May.** May seems to be magical for non-fiction books because a lot of people take time off over the summer to vacation and travel—which leaves them with time to read your book.

Note: Avoid publishing in the last quarter of the year (October, November, or December) *unless* you have a logical reason why, because within ninety days, your book will be last year's book.

Ben here: The timing of your book release has more of an impact than you might think. Do your homework on your genre for answers because it can make the difference between obscurity and the bestseller lists. I've done well from releasing around the holidays, but I also follow a publication calendar throughout the year to prepare for a December release. Knowing your genre and planning your release are key elements in publishing like a boss.

Pro Tip: If your book is poised to solve a problem that coincides with a national holiday, the media is always on the lookout for experts to feature. Subscribe to HARO (Help a Reporter Out) at HelpAReporter.com and receive up to thrice daily emails with media opportunities of every flavor.

How Do I Turn My Book into Multiple Streams of Income?

Ben here: This is a great question and one that has a bearing on your publishing plans. We've talked a lot about how planning ahead can impact the now, and this topic is key. This is because books (especially nonfiction books) can leverage other forms of income. Honorée is incredibly smart on this topic and a perfect example. Her books sell her coaching and her speaking, a synergistic approach that massively magnifies her income. I've learned a great deal from her in this area, and it's helped boost my brand and informed my plans for the future.

You can make money from selling your book one at a time, and that will be amazing! However, you can do several things that will sell multiple copies of your book at a time, *and* you can use the content of your book to make money in multiple ways.

I mention this here because it is important to look at your book and book business as they fit into your other business interests. Ask the question, *How will my book impact my core business?* or *What impact do I want my book to make?* You might even want to design an entire business around your book by repurposing the content into different streams of income.

Honorée here: Here are just a few ways I've multiplied my earnings by increasing how I sell my books and their contents:

Strategy #1: Sell Multiple Copies at Once

Out of all the books I've sold, more than 800,000 of my titles at last count, a good percentage of them have not been sold through Amazon or even as a single book. Quite by accident, I discovered that selling hundreds, thousands, or even tens of thousands of copies to corporate buyers is a real thing and have made it an integral part of my book business.

Mark Victor Hansen, whom I credit with inspiring me to write a book, advised me to ask my clients (and pretty much everyone I knew) to buy between ten and one hundred books (or more). I sold 11,000 copies of *Tall Order!* by selling five, ten, twenty-five, fifty, one hundred, one thousand, and three thousand books at a time—because I asked!

The Successful Single Mom, *The Divorced Phoenix*, and *If Divorce is a Game, These are the Rules* books are purchased by divorce attorneys, CDFAs (certified divorce financial advisors), and even large therapy practices. Why? Because I've allowed (and encouraged!) business professionals to use my book to market their businesses and practices. (See the **Strategy #2**, below.)

When launching your book, you'll want to tell everyone you know in your field about it. It will make sense for them to buy multiple copies when:

- **They don't have their own book.** Handing out a book provides invaluable information to prospective clients. This is something every professional understands; they just don't always understand *how* to do it. At first, give them a copy of your book. When they love it, give them a few copies and suggest they share it. Eventually, offer a mutually-beneficial deal in which they use your book to generate more business for themselves (and you)! Win-win-win.

- **They understand the power of being "front of mind" with complementary service providers.** We all have network connections who serve our ideal client and are not in competition with us. A therapist can pass out a book written by a divorce attorney. A financial advisor can generate new business with a book written by a corporate attorney. Using your book directly with a prospective client can *generate* a client; using your book with other service providers can generate multiple clients, potentially for both the author and the other service provider.

I share these examples because I want you to think of alternate ways to sell your books or get them into the hands of readers who would benefit the most.

Strategy #2: Sell Customized Copies

The back cover of a book is also used as sales copy—wording that is designed to sell the book. When a book is used to grow the business of someone other than the author, the back cover can convert into a business card of sorts. You can turn the back cover of your book into a brochure for the giver. The back covers of these books are customized, and they are called "vanity" copies.

The first time the back cover of *The Successful Single Mom* was customized was for a divorce attorney who wanted to generate more business. He began by leaving copies of my book in Starbucks with his business card because *of course* that's where you go to discuss your impending divorce with your girlfriends! Ladies would stumble on his book, call him for a consultation, and voilà! He had a new client!

After a while, he wanted to customize the book so he didn't need to use his business card and wonder if it had fallen out. I just checked, and to date, he's generated over $15 million in new business as a direct result of buying custom copies of my book. All with an investment of less than $10,000. Not a bad ROI! A business card is a piece of trash waiting to happen, but no one ever throws away a book—they simply pass it on to the next person who needs it.

Another one of my corporate clients added a foil seal to the cover of *Tall Order! ("Compliments of XYZ Company!")* and passed it out to his 3,000 annual convention attendees. He wanted every member of his sales force to "speak the same language," so he created one giant book club—with my book!

Is there a professional who would benefit from purchasing your book with a vanity cover to give out to their strategic partners or prospective clients?

How do I Repurpose My Content?

The content of your book can be the core of a keynote presentation. You can create a training, a workshop, or even a multi-day event. Online courses are gaining in popularity, and while your book will most likely sell for less than $20, a course with audios or even videos, worksheets, and a workbook can command upwards of $1,200 or more. *From the exact same content.*

Here are just a few examples:

Hal Elrod, my partner and the author of *The Miracle Morning* series, gives a keynote presentation for $25,000. His speech shares the principles in his book, which he combines with stories and humor. His presentations sell more books, which in turn generate more speaking engagements. In addition, his books, the book series, and his keynotes drive readers to attend his annual *Best Year Ever* event in San Diego each December.

I've turned my book *Vision to Reality* into a popular keynote I charge a nice sum to deliver. I also have a course that walks attendees through their 100-day challenge with audio and other extras. That $400 course sells several times a month, and I offer discounts in my various other books and newsletters. For about five years, I've charged $2,500 per person to coach groups of six professionals through their 100-day challenge. That book alone has earned me over $1 million in multiple revenue streams.

You can use the content of your book to provide consulting, coaching, or speaking services or even to start a podcast (which you can eventually monetize with sponsorships and ads). I'm fully aware that each of these requires *more* of your time. Your time will come at a premium as an author—you'll be able to charge more for your products or services the moment you're published.

Ben here: Are you feeling daunted? Don't worry! We're just trying to show you options. It's up to you to choose the ones that work best for you. What you're seeing is years of experiences compiled into a single book. Notice how Honorée has used one technique to grow and build into another. If you are feeling overwhelmed, I'd suggest making a list of these ideas and take note of the ones that seem like a good starting point. Then identify the ones you might want to grow into later. Knowing what you want in the future helps shape your now.

Honorée here: Want to spend less time and still have multiple streams of income? Consider the course avenue discussed above. You can also create a companion guide, journal, agenda, or workbook. You can record audios of the lessons and information you provide in your book and charge a small (or large!) fee for a download, and encourage your listeners to take them to the gym or listen during their daily commute. These are just a few ways to repurpose the core content of your book. There is no limit to how many ways you can monetize your repurposed content.

The Ultimate Sign of a Pro

To make my books indistinguishable from traditionally-published books, I've carefully looked at hundreds of different books and added these subtle yet essential details:

On the cover:

- **A publishing company logo.** You'll want to commission a logo for your publishing company. You can establish a separate company from your core business, or you can add "Publishing" or "Publications" to your core business name. Your logo can look similar or completely different. There's no right or wrong here, just what makes fiscal and reasonable sense. The placement of the logo is at the bottom of the spine under the author name or above the title.

- **A photo and bio.** Readers have expressed that being able to see my face made them feel more connected, and in some instances encouraged their purchase.

- **A company URL.** Readers want to find out more, and your URL can help make that easy. On your website, they'll learn more about what you do and how you can help them.

- **Book categories.** List the main categories for your book, such as Family & Relationships / Dating or Business / Money.

- **Pricing.** Include the prices in the US and Canada.

- **The actual ISBN**. In addition to the barcode, include your book's ISBN.

Inside the book.

- **An interior page that mimics the cover.** This page is the first page inside the front cover.

- **Praise for the book.** This page goes next. Gather enough endorsements to fill the front and back of one page. Third-party validation means a lot, especially since the number one way readers find a book is through a personal recommendation.

- **Also by the author.** If you have other books or publications, include a list (no matter how short!) on its own page.

- **Your book's information page.** This page includes the publisher's note, copyright information, the ISBN numbers for all editions, and copyright protection. You'll also include credits for the book. List who did your cover design, interior layout, editing, and proofreading (and their respective websites, if you're able and feeling especially generous).

I've owned two publishing companies: Leading Edge Publishing, LLC (when I lived in Nevada), and—since that company name was taken when I moved to Texas—Honorée Enterprises Publishing, LLC.

Why establish a separate company? For a couple of reasons! First, you expect to earn significant revenues from your book, and a separate company helps to pave the way by setting that expectation in your mind. Second, a fully-formed company provides protections in the event someone decides to target you wrongly. They will be forced to sue the entity that owns the information contained in the book, instead of litigating against you personally or your other business(es).

Final Advice on Your Nonfiction Book

One of the things I've always tried to do is write a book that is evergreen, meaning it's relevant now and (almost) forever. For example, you might be tempted to write a book about how to invest in the stock market in 2017, but soon that book will be out of date and useless (and therefore will no longer sell). You would be better off writing a book about sound money strategies useful in any market, and then use a dozen examples of how to invest in different types of markets, whether the economy is doing well or not.

Make sense?

When choosing your book's topic, write about something that will be useful to readers now and in the future. Just like with your brand, you are better off thinking long-term. A time-sensitive book is like an avocado—it's terrific, but if you don't consume it within a few days, you'll end up throwing it away.

I hope you've learned enough that you're excited to get started on your book. The next chapter focuses on the resources we both use to help manage the business, so grab a fresh cup of joe, settle in, and turn the page.

5

RESOURCES

onorée here: As much information as we have given you, it's just the tip of the iceberg. We could write a thousand-page book to cover everything, but you probably only need a few pieces of information. Instead, this chapter is devoted to guiding you in the right direction in the future. *Publish Like a Boss* is intended as a starting point, and hopefully by now you know what questions you need to ask for your business. But where to go for answers? Here you go:

AUTHOR EARNINGS REPORT

We've talked about this site before, but now we get to talk about how truly incredible it is. Over the last few years, they have released data that is mind-blowing, showing market trends that are essential to any author. One of their more memorable reports studied the last two and a half years, and the graphs are shocking. Another, from June 2017, studied one million titles, going into detail on who is making money on Amazon.

The information on Author Earnings Report is invaluable in making decisions for the future. As we said at the beginning, to *Publish Like a Boss*, you must study your market, and this site is your university. Even the older reports (and by old, I mean two years ago!) are incredibly informative.

FACEBOOK

Most regard Facebook as a social site, but for professionals, it's a place of business. Everything from marketing to group meetings occurs daily. There are hundreds of groups dedicated to writers of all types. Seek out and join the groups where you can both learn and contribute.

Indie Writers Unite is one of my favorite groups. You'll have to request to join, and they let in most authors. They do not permit advertising, so if you post a link to your website, you could get kicked out (and permanently). But if you have a question about formatting, marketing, or writing, chances are you'll find someone in the group with an answer. Experience levels range from pre-publication to full-time, six-figure-earning authors.

Of course, I'd love you to join my Facebook community, The Prosperous Writer Mastermind. I offer a positive, inclusive environment where *all* questions (as well as shameless self-promotion) are welcome. If one of your focus areas is money and increasing your prosperity consciousness, we'd love to have you!

SUBCONTRACTORS

As a writer, there are several subcontractors you are likely going to need. Cover designer, editor, proofreader, book coach, beta readers, and more are all potential parts of a writing and publishing process. You may already have access to some of these or feel like you can skip others, but it's important to know how to find them and how to work with them.

Freelance editors are becoming much more common, and they frequently can be found where authors congregate. Talk to any published author and chances are they have an editor recommendation. You can ask in the Facebook groups you've joined or at in-person writing groups. Either way, make sure the editor you choose is a professional. A quality edit on a 100,000-word fantasy novel should cost you $1,000–$2,000, depending on complexity and the clarity of the text. And yes, it's worth the investment. A good editor can raise your reviews by a full star—or more. Ask about their process and their schedule, as well as their rates.

Great info, Ben, and I agree. Nonfiction editors, great ones, are getting easier to find because traditional publishers need fewer of them. There are many folks with great editing chops that are available, but you'll have to book them well in advance (just as in any profession, people with the best skills aren't sitting around waiting for work—they are booked weeks and possibly months in advance).

I like to work with editors who consider themselves "word nerds" and who have a background in traditional publishing. It is important to find an editor whose style works with yours—I like to work with friendly editors who encourage me to write with abandon, knowing they will follow me and make my words into a fun, smooth read. Be sure to get solid references and have a conversation or two to make sure they are the right fit. If someone makes you feel bad, they aren't the editor for you. There are plenty out there, so keep asking for referrals and interviewing until you find just the right person for your team.

The more experienced the editor, the more they will charge. While fees aren't always an indicator of skill and experience, be wary of someone who is cheap (and see my section addressing the same earlier in this book).

Pro Tip: **(Ben here)** Remember that there are different types of editors. Some are developmental; others are copyeditors. Make sure you are getting the one you need for your book. Also, keep in mind that the relationship between a writer and an editor is like any other job. It doesn't always click at first.

Covers

As you prepare your book for publication, let's talk about how to get a great cover. The most important realization is this: your cover is not part of your book. It's part of your brand.

Most authors gravitate toward a cover that represents the book, but that can be a costly mistake. You want a cover that draws people to the book. The difference may seem negligible but can have an enormous impact on your sales.

Color schemes, layout, text styles, and theme all need to be considered. You want a cover that works for digital as well as print (and yes, they have different needs). The place to start is the place your readers buy books. If it's Amazon, go to the bestseller list and browse the top 100. What catches your eye? What stands out? Do you see any themes?

Covers that tend to stand out are impactful and straightforward, and they evoke an emotion. Nonfiction books might evoke curiosity, ambition, or excitement. Fiction covers might evoke a sense of fantasy, desire, or fear. These feelings help turn browsers into readers.

Good cover designers are usually not your nephew who is a great artist. Graphic designers charge anywhere from $200 to $2,000 a cover, or higher if they have a great reputation. Digital artists (like those that draw the artwork for fantasy covers) are even more. They will set you back $500–$2,500. That might sound like a lot of money, but keep in mind that without the investment in the brand, readers will be less interested in your book.

Honorée here: Like I said earlier, your book never gets a second chance to make a first impression, and the first impression you want your book to make is "Read me!" And you do that by having a professional cover that is clear, conveys the subject matter or genre of the book, and makes your prospective reader want more.

LEGAL AND STUFF

A lot of authors want to get their work copyrighted, and for a good reason: a copyright protects your intellectual property and records you as the owner of record. The good news is that the process is simple and does not require an attorney. But obtaining a copyright isn't the only thing for which you'll need the services of an excellent attorney.

Contracts can be convoluted and confusing. Traditional publishing houses typically request the "worldwide rights for the life of the copyright." Translation: they want all the rights to your content until seventy years after you die. And by all, I mean all. They want the rights to digital books, print books, audio books, television, film, foreign, games, video games, and anything else that might pop up now and in the future. If your book takes off in sales and popularity, they will own the rights, not you. And this is just one line in a contract that, at first read, doesn't stand out as particularly important. Do yourself a huge favor and talk to an attorney before signing any contract.

Better still, interview business and intellectual property attorneys before you need them. As soon as possible (yesterday, if not sooner), find an attorney to talk to about your book business. Explain what you write and how often you publish (or plan to publish), and under no circumstances do you sign anything without your attorney giving it a twice-over. I've used my attorney for seven years, and I cannot even begin to calculate the amount of money, time, energy, and aggravation he's helped me avoid (as well as ensuring my book business is continuously successful)!

If you write books with other authors, agree to publish a book with a publisher of any type, or even accept a speaking engagement, you need to have an Agreement. Unless you're an attorney, make sure you have one on your team (and be sure to listen to their advice)!

ISBN

ISBNs are another thing you'll want to understand. These numbers are used to identify your book and are required on all print editions and highly recommended for ebooks as well (although not legally required). The iBookstore and Sony actually require the numbers on ebooks.

You can purchase ISBNs from Bowkers (http://www.myidentifiers.com); the cost will vary. An individual ISBN is $125, a hefty price tag when you consider that different editions can't share an ISBN. You'll have to use a different one for each print and ebook. Buying ten ISBNs costs $295, and a block of one hundred (which is how we purchase our ISBNs) costs $575. It's up to you which you buy, but consider the options before you spend the cash.

If you're publishing any book in both ebook and paperback, you already need two ISBNs. If, like us, you get the book-writing bug, you'll want to write more books. It is worth it to invest in purchasing a block of one hundred ISBNs, as you'll end up spending more than that even if you only ever publish three books. Consider it the cost of doing business, and in this case, each ISBN only costs $5.75 (which is much more palatable than $125).

Additionally, having those ISBNs with no books attached to them should inspire you to write more!

Writing Groups

Ben here: My first writing group was great. At the time, I had one finished book and was just learning how bad it was. Attending the writing group helped me learn to channel criticism into improvement. I can attribute much of my early growth to that group and remember it with fondness. There are a few types of writing groups, and each serves a different purpose. In *Write Like a Boss*, we touched on critique groups, but there is another type that deserves mention here.

Writing groups are everywhere! When you reach a certain point in your career, you aren't looking for writing help. You're looking for publishing help. This is where writers' guilds and associations become useful.

These organizations frequently have conferences, with speakers drawn from agents, published authors, and industry professionals. Going to the larger conferences, as well as the smaller events, gives you the opportunity to learn in a way that's difficult to do online. I would have given a lot to learn from Honorée back then!

I've seen speakers talk about the science of crime for mystery writers, the craft of world building, and the art of a book cover. Some of the elements I've talked about in this book I learned from great speakers in the Florida Writer's Association, one of the more prodigious writer's organizations in the United States. Look around for a good writer's group to join so you can learn, and perhaps one day you'll be the speaker.

GETTING ANSWERS

I like to think of publishing like a five-level pyramid. At the base, you have all the new authors just launching their books or finishing their manuscripts. The next level up, the authors have a few books out and are just beginning to understand the industry. Third-tier authors have more knowledge and are comfortable in many respects, perhaps even approaching the coveted full-time mark. Most fourth-tier writers are full-time or close to it, not due to sales, but due to experience. They have detailed knowledge of every facet of the industry. Fifth-tiers know it all (or most of it, anyway), and their hard work has built a vast wealth of knowledge.

Connecting with fifth-tier, *New York Times* bestselling authors is great, but they might not be able to help you if you are in the first or second tier. That's because the challenges they face are vastly different from yours. Look to interact with the authors at your level or one level above you. Doing so allows you to find quality answers that are relevant to you. Honorée and I love to connect with new authors and talk about writing. But our schedules are full, and you might not get the answer when you need it the most. But as you build a network of peers, you'll find a wealth of collective information. Many of these writers will grow with you, forming the foundation of your future network. Now, I'm not saying you can't talk to authors that are further along than you are in your career. You can, and should, connect with authors of every type. But when looking to build your career, learn to identify those who will be most helpful to you and begin building a relationship in a slow and steady way as soon as possible! (You'll want to pick up Honorée's book, *Business Dating*, which lays out an entire process for making that happen almost effortlessly.)

6

THE BASICS OF MARKETING

Ben here: Although we cover each of these topics in detail in *Market Like a Boss*, there are a few things you should consider while publishing. Each of these topics is enormous, and it will take time for you to learn them all. However, like the rest of this book, we want you to know how to *Publish Like a Boss*, and to do that, you must know the basics of book marketing (and when to start marketing your upcoming books).

FINDING YOUR BRAND

We've already talked about how to make a great cover, but here we'd like to go into a bit more detail about how it's part of your brand.

Whether you consider it to be the case or not, the moment you hit publish, you are launching your brand. Readers will learn to associate the style, composition, text, and color with you. That can be good or bad, depending on what your choices are communicating with your readers and how that aligns with your brand.

I've met an author who swears, drinks, smokes, and tells filthy jokes. His readers love him for it, and to clean up his speech would be off-brand for him. I've met another author who writes erotic fiction, and her brand is funny and crass. For her, that's on-brand, and her covers reflect that.

Early on, I made the mistake of approaching writing like a traditional profession and even went to writing groups in a full suit. As I grew comfortable with my brand, I relaxed to a more casual personality (coincidently the more natural one for me). I've even worn—dare I say it—a t-shirt to a book signing. I write clean fiction and like to encourage others, but am not above a little fun. With a bit of encouragement, you might even get me to break dance (I know, I wouldn't believe it either). Overall, this brand fits me much better.

Another aspect of branding is choosing whether to write under a pen name. You might be thinking that a pen name will shield you, and to a certain extent, that's true. But a pen name is its own brand, complete with how you post on social media, how you present your books, even how your pen name "looks."

The point is this: the brand you create starts with your covers. Are your nonfiction titles sharp and clean? Or funny and witty?

Honorée here: I'm with Ben and agree that your author brand is communicated in every piece of your presence. I aim to communicate smart, competent, and knowledgeable, as well as fun, authentic, and approachable. These six words inform and influence each aspect of my book business. From my social media posts to the content of my books, and even what I wear to the post office or speaking engagements (hint: the post office gets "dressy casual," and speaking engagements vary between "professional chic" to "Wall Street banker" depending on my audience).

Most importantly, you need to feel confident and comfortable with your brand, because that's when you'll both be at your best.

Ben here: Publishing a book is taking a step into the public eye. Your book is an extension of you and your brand. Be sure it reflects the brand you want, or you may regret it later (or wish you had taken more time to think it through). In addition, think ahead to what you want to write. Is it part of your brand? Is your new book going to enhance or deviate from that brand? These are the questions you should be asking when you are working with a designer on your cover. They are working for you, so if they don't know what your goals are, how can they do their job?

Ben hits the nail on the head here—you can always ramp up your brand, but reining it in is harder. Going from Hannah Montana to the Miley Cyrus we saw on a wrecking ball was a distinct change. It has taken quite a bit of work on her part to again view her as a respectable, serious musician. Angelina Jolie is still fighting against her earlier, more risqué performances as she has matured into more substantive roles.

Publishing like a boss means beginning with the end in mind, and sometimes it's hard to imagine an empire when you're first getting started and only have a book (or five) under your belt. Take time to reflect and figure out where you'd like your book business to be in five years' time, and that vision will help you make crucial decisions today.

Social Media Platform

Ben here: Before we talk about the merits of social media, let me point out something important. Publishing will bring you into the public world, meaning anything you've posted on any site will eventually be connected to you and your brand. Posting on controversial topics is your right, but it may anger those who feel differently than you. While you are a private citizen, there's not much readers (or haters) could do to harm you. When you are published, they can (and some will) review your book negatively, organize campaigns against you, and even attempt to sway readers away from your books. I'm not going to discourage or encourage you to post anything, but you should consider the ramifications of your social media platform, especially if it differs from the author persona you want to create.

Ben is right—you have a right to your opinion. But those who oppose your viewpoint *can* choose to disagree with you in the form of a one-star review of your book! The three hot topics to avoid if you want to avoid controversy are *religion, sex*, and *politics*. While I do have strong opinions on almost every subject imaginable (I know, shocking, right?), unless we're *super close* you won't ever know what they are as I hold them close to the vest. Keeping an air of neutrality around you will allow others to express themselves freely, and it's always a great thing for others to feel comfortable in your presence. An exception is if you are okay with writing or talking about those three subjects—then dive in with your eyes wide open.

Ben here: Now, on to the good stuff. Social media marketing is virtually a must in today's world, and the topic is huge. For now, let's talk about creating the foundation of your social media marketing efforts.

First up: Facebook.

You'll most likely want to create a Facebook page with the title of your series or your name as an author. A page (versus a profile) allows you to interact with readers without them requesting to be your friend. You may not want them to see pictures of your kids or family, but you do want them to know about your new book or book signings or other special events. We'll talk about Facebook marketing in detail later (and a whole lot in *Market Like a Boss*), but for now, creating a page is a start. Make sure the banner image is sharp (could be an image featuring your book's cover) and that you occasionally (if not consistently) post.

Other Options.

Twitter and Instagram are two other platforms that authors use regularly. I should say that I don't have an Instagram account. The reason for this is that I want to focus my efforts on Facebook, with a little on Twitter. Having a presence on social media sites allows readers who frequent those sites to find you. Don't make it hard for readers to track you down.

Honorée here: I also have a presence on Facebook, including a personal page, an author page, and the Prosperous Writer Mastermind. I also *love* Instagram, so I'm on there quite a bit. I use Twitter sparingly. Here's why: I've found that when someone discovers an author's work, they go looking for them online (I do it, don't you?). If your goal is to build a solid author brand and have a large platform, people have to be able to find you easily.

Enter: Chris Syme's *Sell More Books with Less Social Media*. In her book (which I highly recommend!), she shows how to make the most of every minute you spend on social media. And yes, Ben is spot-on (of course)— he's spending his time, as am I, where most everyone spends their time these days: *on Facebook*. While you'll need to read her book to understand her philosophy and integrate it into your overall brand-building, very simply you want anyone who looks for you to find you easily. Then you tell them where to go to find out more.

Your Website

The first place I go when I discover a person I want to know more about is my search bar. I type in "theirname.com" and see what pops up. A true professional has their name (or their book series or company name) for their website.

While you can, and should, spend time on social media, one thing is clear: all platforms evolve (Facebook is continuously expanding), and some go away entirely (MySpace, anyone?). While it is great to connect with new readers and fans on social media, ultimately you must have a hub that is your own, and a website is perfect! You control the content, brand, and message, and you can take your relationship with readers to the next level (more on that next), and even sell your books.

Ben here: It's essential that you have a website, blog, or both when you publish. Fans may look for your online presence, and if they can't find you, they might assume you aren't a professional.

There are plenty of places you can create a free blog. After all you've invested in editing, cover design, and ISBNs, a free blog sounds good, right? It did to me. I'd invested $5,000 into editing and cover design and didn't want to spend any more on a website. I created a free blog on Blogger and began posting. The site probably looked terrible, but it was my first foray into the public domain. A year later, my books had taken off, and I invested the time to create a WordPress site. Two years after that, I invested even more into a more robust site, www.Lumineia.com.

It's not perfect, but it has many of the elements readers want out of an author's website.

Honorée here: Ben offers a great beginning option. It is fine to use free services and platforms when you're getting started. Keep in mind (and prepare by saving up, if you don't have the capital you need right now!) that eventually you should invest in a custom website (or at least a semi-custom templated website). As a legit business, you must have a legit website. You wouldn't wear flip-flops and shorts to a black-tie wedding, and the web is a virtual black-tie wedding. Dress your website accordingly! (The same rule applies to your books, too!)

The Subscriber List

Ben here: Another aspect of professional publishing (and building your author brand) is your list of subscribers. Readers who like your work want more, and a subscriber list is a great way to stay in touch. We'll talk about how to grow your list in *Market Like a Boss*. For the purposes of publishing, it's enough just to create one and begin to collect subscribers. There are a handful of free services you can employ that will remain free up to a certain number of subscribers. MailChimp and AWeber are two popular options to consider.

The reason this is part of publishing is the time it takes for a list to mature. Unfortunately, I didn't know much about subscriber lists when I started out. (No one had written *Publish Like a Boss*!) It took me two years to learn about a subscriber list and add that page to my website. Although I was late to the game, my list now has almost 1,500 people, enough to make a big impact on sales when I have a new release.

Just imagine the power of your subscriber list when you have 5,000 people wanting to know when you have a book release. Keep in mind that only a portion of those will be buyers, but even if just 100 subscribers buy your book the day it releases, that's enough to shoot you high enough in the rankings to gain a bit of traction.

I use MailChimp. It's free up to a certain threshold, and the system is robust and easy to learn. Feel free to consider multiple options before you pick one, and make sure to do so *before* you publish your book. Adding a page with an option to join your newsletter or to download a free book or short story will give your readers a place to go when they finish reading!

If you're looking for examples of what to include in your first email or email series, sign up for other authors' lists. You'll receive their emails and start to figure out what you like (and what you don't!). Don't copy, not just because it's not right, but because you can't copy their brand. You are developing your own brand, and using inspiration from others can surely help.

Honorée here: I waited years too long to begin building my list. Because I write on several nonfiction topics, I have multiple lists (business, writing, single parents, and divorce). I use (and adore) AWeber because it offers sophisticated capabilities while remaining easy to use.

I grow each list by offering something in exchange for an email address. I give away free books, two chapters of several books, tools I mention in my books, and resource lists. I would much rather have a subscriber with whom I can build a relationship than a single book sale. I *love* my readers and always personally answer each email (even if it takes me a little time to do so). We'll do a deep dive into growing your list and incorporating your list into your book marketing in *Market Like a Boss*.

BOOKMARKS & OTHER PRINTED MATTER

Ben here: When you publish, you're going to want to tell your friends, and nothing says writer like a bookmark. They are inexpensive and act as your business card. Good ones show the link to your website and your cover. I prefer mini-bookmarks, which are business-card sized and easy to fit into a wallet. Regardless of your choice, make sure you do some planning. Printing and shipping take time, and remember you only get increased exposure from online retailers for a limited time. Make sure to maximize the time to the fullest by adding your own additional promotion.

Honorée here: Bookmarks are great—I use them as well. You can even have business cards disguised as bookmarks. The sky is the limit with what you can have printed to share with potential readers and contacts. I share lots of fun ideas in *The Prosperous Writer's Guide to Finding Readers*.

CONFERENCES

Ben here: With the rise of indie publishing, a second industry has appeared: indie cons (the common term for conferences). These conferences cater to all indie authors, from those with only one book to those who have dozens. I went to my first con in my second year. At the time, I had four books published but only one in print. I brought thirty books and stacked them all on the table, hoping to fill empty space. I didn't have bookmarks, pens, shirts, or other swag. I didn't have posters or special tablecloths, and I didn't sell well. I count myself lucky to sell just two copies, netting myself a grand total of $4 for an event that cost nearly $400.

Honorée here: Ben brings up a good point. I had no idea cons existed until almost a decade into my writing career. A friend of mine recommended I listen to Steve Scott on the James Altucher Show ("He makes a ton of money self-publishing, just like you!"), and that podcast led me to the Self-Publishing Podcast, which led me to my first con ... and the rest is history. I've now written a half-dozen books with authors I could only have met at a writer's conference. Almost no one in publishing talks about the true value of a network, but just as in traditional businesses, your success comes down to *who you know*. The more author friends and connections you have, the greater your chances of success.

Why? Because other writers and authors have the knowledge you need. Because your author buddies understand your business and can offer support and encouragement. Because knowing you're not alone is *awesome*.

The best place to find and connect with your future writer network is at conferences. Writers who attend conferences are people who invest in themselves and their craft. Even if this is your first week as a writer (and you just happen to pick up this book or series), you should have an eye toward finding other folks just like you! (And welcome, by the way. We're a fun crowd!) In *Market Like a Boss*, you'll learn how to leverage your network. Hint: build your network before you need it, from a place of authenticity. Why? Because true friends are thrilled to help when asked—the best of friends will take it upon themselves to help and ask you how they can. A solid network of other writers is invaluable, and the sooner you start building it, the better!

Okay, so we've covered the basics of marketing because it's never too soon to start! We'll cover the aspects you'll need to be successful over the long term in *Marketing Like a Boss*, but before you can truly dive into marketing, you must have something to market.

7

HITTING PUBLISH

Ben here: I remember the moment I hit "publish" for my very first novel. It was the last day of May, 2012, and I was nervous but excited. At the time, indie publishing was very new, with little information on the topic. I talked to my friends in my writing group, other authors who were indie published, and anyone I could find. But information was scarce.

I remember the feeling of venturing into a new industry. Untested and still fragile, it seemed the world of indie publishing had all the promise and wonder of an adventure. My first day, I sold two copies, and to this day I think they were to my wife and my mother. But the next day I sold another two, and one on the third day. On the fifth day, I sold four copies, and I was ecstatic. I couldn't believe what was happening. Who was buying them? Surely my mom wasn't buying a book a day to make me feel good. Then who? Friends, relatives or, dare I believe it, actual readers?

Sales gradually ticked upward until the first week of July, when I was averaging five sales a day. Then I had a birthday and several of my friends bought my books. I didn't know it at the time, but the ten extra sales bumped my ranking onto a bestseller list.

I stared at that screen for several minutes, shocked to see my book on a bestseller list. It wasn't a big one, mind you, but it was selling, and people wanted to read it. My wife claimed she always knew. I claimed it was just a fluke. But deep down I was terrified of believing my book could sell.

I did my first promotion later that month, giving my book out for free. Looking back, there were several things I did wrong, but because I did my research, I did several things right, and my book continued to climb. At this point, it was selling almost twenty-five copies a day, and I made nearly $1,000 in August.

My book dominated my thoughts, seeping into odd moments of the day, sparking thrills of excitement followed by gripping fear. Was it about to end? Had it run its course?

It turns out it had. I got my first negative review, a scathing two-star review that sent my book into a free fall. Within a month, my book went from selling thirty copies a day to three, and I was devastated. Truth be told, I was also a little angry. But I was all set to publish book two (I had already written three) and hit "publish." This time I did with a great deal of trepidation. Would it climb in the rankings? Or suffer the same fate as book one?

To my relief and renewed excitement, my new book pulled the first out of obscurity, and in three weeks they were both selling twenty-five copies a day. If the sales were all from my mom, she was doing great.

Early December, I published book three to complete the trilogy, and my sales skyrocketed. By the end of the year, my first book was selling one hundred and fifty books a day, and the sequels were averaging one hundred each. I decided to leverage the momentum for more, sold my business and went all in, writing three more books the next year. My sales plummeted shortly after, but I wrote enough to weather the dip and managed to endure until the following year. And I've never looked back.

That was my journey. I did research, I studied, I studied more, but I couldn't be prepared for the one thing I wanted: success. Writing full-time had a whole world of problems, but I knew what I wanted to do, so I tackled them with all the zeal of the naïve, and I persevered. By the end of 2017, I'll have published more than twenty books, three of which will be with Honorée.

I hit my five-year mark as a full-time writer in June and took a moment to marvel at what had occurred. I work hard writing, editing, and learning, and I love my job. But it all started with the simple courage to hit "publish."

Writing full-time is a dream of many, and I sometimes wonder why I managed to accomplish it. I think it has a great deal to do with my attitude toward the business. I didn't let ignorance or fear derail me; I sought to learn and gathered my courage. I've had thousands of moments where I thought it was over, that my books had run their course. But I refused to give up, to let my dream fall by the wayside. You shouldn't either!

Honorée here: I published for the first time in 2004—*Tall Order!* was published under a different title (long and horrible), different cover (it's so bad it would hurt your eyes!), and no editing (I know, *I know*). I didn't know what I didn't know (a.k.a. pretty much everything in this book). Thankfully, Jeffrey Gitomer crossed my path, and the rest is history.

I immediately spruced up my book, and as I mentioned, got busy selling it to every person in my (ahem) Rolodex (youngsters, you'll know this as the contacts in your phone), my friends, family, clients, and pretty much anyone I'd meet. Being an author is cool, remember? As soon as I got a few dopamine rushes that accompanied someone *else* getting excited about my book, I was hooked!

Because I didn't know what I didn't know, I didn't let fear stop me. I didn't have any brain static, or head noise, or self-doubts. I should have, mind you, but I didn't. I'm glad I didn't, and here's why: If I had had any doubts and had let them stand in my way, I wouldn't be sitting on my couch in my stretchy pants with a hot cup of tea and a cat on my lap doing what I love *for a living*. I have no idea what I'd be doing, but I'm sure I wouldn't love it as much as being a writer (and speaker and coach). I love almost every single minute of my life, and that wouldn't have happened if I had let anything stand in my way.

I didn't even try traditional publishing because I definitely wouldn't have called myself a writer or an author. It never occurred to me to seek an agent or try to get a publishing deal, not even when I got the idea to write *The Successful Single Mom*. I knew a few other authors who published their own books (Jeffrey Gitomer and James Malinchak were just two I knew personally) and so I didn't give it much thought.

What can you take away from my story? I'd love you to consider this:

Your book can never be as bad as mine. Just kidding—but not really; it was bad. In all seriousness, *published* is better than unpublished! *Get it out into the world.* Then, and only then, can you receive feedback that will truly be helpful. You might hear it's great! You might also hear it needs more work, more editing, more stories (nonfiction), or a better story (fiction). A finished first book can be made better, if necessary (that's why I released the 10th Anniversary Edition of *Tall Order!* in 2015). Alternatively, you can take what you learned and write your next book.

Whether you have to give yourself a hard publication date or commit to just *one more pass* before you hit publish, at some point, you have to draw an immovable line in the sand. Set a hard deadline, commit to do whatever it takes to get it done, and then just do it!

Is a lack of self-confidence holding you back from publishing? You're not alone! There is no better time than today to begin to quiet your monkey mind with a steady stream of motivation and inspiration. Here are a few books and programs to get you started:

- *The Miracle Morning* by Hal Elrod
- *The Power of Consistency* by Weldon Long
- *What to Say When You Talk to Yourself* by Shad Helmstetter
- *Think & Grow Rich* by Napoleon Hill
- *The Prosperous Writer* series by me
- "Unleash the Power Within" seminar by Tony Robbins
- PSI Basic Seminar (PsiSeminars.com)

Ben here: I would add to this list, but everything I've read is here. (And a few I haven't!) These will be great additional resources to you as you look for more information.

My dad always said that any time you step into a new venture, you pay the Dumb Tax, meaning you lose money because of dumb mistakes. Looking back, there are plenty of mistakes on my backlist and business. But as we said in *Write Like a Boss*, learning is part of the business. Using the resources you have will help to mitigate the Dumb Tax. Don't pay extra taxes!

Honorée here: Your level of success will seldom exceed your level of self-development. If you don't already have a solid personal-improvement program in place, you won't go wrong by developing one. What does this have to do with publishing? Well, there is a huge contingent of writers who want to be authors, but hold themselves back from publishing their books because they don't believe their book is good enough—or that *they* are good enough!

You can fool yourself into thinking you need more revisions, more editions, one more proofread, a different ending, more research, or countless other things that may or may not be true (they're probably not). If you want to achieve a good balance and counteract limiting beliefs, your best bet is to work on yourself.

A healthy self-esteem allows for you to make logical, objective decisions about your work. Said another way, you will think of your book as you would any other product or service. Your book is *not* your "baby," nor is it an extension of yourself to be used as yet another way to judge yourself in a negative way.

Fiction or nonfiction, a book—your book—is simply one of your creations. Like a pie. Or a legal brief. Or an email. When it's time to put the pie in the oven, you do it! You don't hang on to it for six extra months, marinating on whether or not to bake it, right? You do the best you can, and if it comes out less than perfect, you don't beat yourself up. You simply bake another pie.

Your pie is obviously your book. Do the best you can, and then release it to the world—come what may! Who knows? You might just have the next international sensation on your hands!

Side note: My original book, still listed on Amazon by a third-party seller, is currently ranked an impressively low 17,269,531. I didn't even know an item could be ranked that low! See? I told you yours could never be as bad as mine!

Ben here: Do you want to be a writer? Then be one. But it's more than just writing. This fantastic, troubled, vast, daunting, wondrous, scary, friendly, awesome world of publishing is so much more than putting words on a page. Writing and publishing are entirely different pursuits, with entirely different learning curves and entirely different skills. But you can learn to *Publish Like a Boss*.

The fact that you are reading this book is good, and I hope you've taken pages of notes on what you want to do with your career. But if you want to be great, use this book as a launching point. Learn how to publish and keep learning, because reaching your dream of writing full-time requires a master's degree in publishing. And if you put the information in this book into practice, you've just finished your first semester.

If you write fiction, you know the main character will grow from the journey and conflict they face. Well, this is your story, the tale of an aspiring novelist or author to full-time author and bestseller. I know you can do this because I did it. Stack the odds in your favor and no matter what, keep writing.

You stand on a wonderful precipice. I urge you to take the plunge and get ready to publish. Whatever your genre, whatever your purpose, the world will be better with your voice. Be relentless in learning. Be relentless in writing. Be relentless in Publishing—Like a Boss.

QUICK FAVOR

━━━━━━━━━━━━━━━━━━━━━━━━━
━━━━━━━━━━━━━━━━━━━━━━━━━

We're wondering, did you enjoy this book?

First of all, thank you for reading our book! May we ask a quick favor?

Will you take a moment to leave an honest review for this book? Reviews are the BEST way to help others purchase the book.

You can go to the link below and write your thoughts. We appreciate you!

HonoreeCorder.com/PublishLABreview

WHO IS HONORÉE?

Honorée Corder is the author of dozens of books, including the *Like a Boss* book series, *You Must Write a Book, I Must Write My Book, The Prosperous Writer Book Series, Vision to Reality, Business Dating, The Successful Single Mom* book series, *If Divorce is a Game, These are the Rules,* and *The Divorced Phoenix.*

She is also Hal Elrod's business partner in *The Miracle Morning* book series. Honorée coaches business professionals, writers, and aspiring nonfiction authors who want to publish their books to bestseller status, create a platform, and develop multiple streams of income. She also does all sorts of other magical things, and her badassery is legendary. You can find out more at HonoréeCorder.com.

Honorée Enterprises, Inc.
Honorée@HonoréeCorder.com
http://www.HonoréeCorder.com
Twitter: @Honorée
& @Singlemombooks
Facebook: http://www.facebook.com/Honorée

WHO IS BEN?

B en Hale is the best-selling author of the Chronicles of Lumineia. Originally from Utah, Ben grew up with a passion for learning. Drawn particularly to reading, he was caught reading by flashlight under the covers at a young age. While still young, he practiced various sports, became an Eagle Scout, and taught himself to play the piano. This thirst for knowledge gained him excellent grades and helped him graduate college with honors, as well as become fluent in three languages after doing volunteer work in Brazil. After school, he started and ran several successful businesses that gave him time to work on his numerous writing projects.

Ben launched his first book in 2012, and six months later he sold his business and began writing full-time. Since then he has published 17 titles across five series within the fantasy world of Lumineia. To date his series has sold 200,000 copies and continues to garner praise from readers. His greatest support comes from his wonderful wife and six beautiful children. Currently he resides in Missouri while working on his Masters in Professional Writing.

To contact Ben, discover more about Lumineia, or find out about upcoming sequels, check out his website at Lumineia.com. You can also follow him on twitter @BenHale8 or Facebook.